A HISTORY OF GREECE

GREECE IN THE FIFTH CENTURY B.C.

A HISTORY OF GREECE

BY

E. FEARENSIDE, M.A.

LATE SCHOLAR OF QUEEN'S COLLEGE, OXFORD

London and Edinburgh:

T. C. & E. C. JACK, LTD. | T. NELSON & SONS, LTD.

1919

CONTENTS

GREECE AND THE

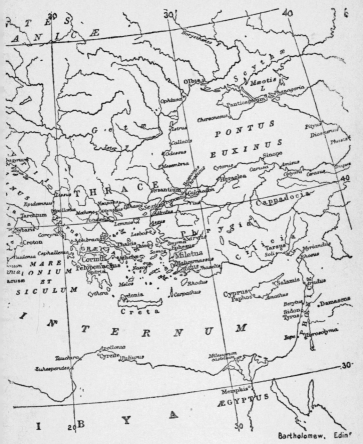

GREEK COLONIES.

A HISTORY OF GREECE.

INTRODUCTORY.

THE great principle of Western civilisation, as distinct from Eastern, is that of liberty, with all that it implies—freedom of thought and of action, and the consequent development of politics, art, literature, philosophy. This principle we find first taking root and flourishing amongst the Greeks: they first create a distinctively European civilisation, and then maintain it against the aggression of Persia in the East and Carthage in the West at the time of the great Persian wars; gradually they extend their influence over their rougher and less cultured neighbours. Greek civilisation triumphed with Macedon over Persia, and, in a sense, with Rome over Carthage, so that eventually the whole Mediterranean basin, especially the eastern half, was permeated by Greek influence.

The achievements of Greece in the realm of thought —that literature and art that have served as models for all subsequent ages in Europe—have no place here; the aim of this book is briefly to relate their political history, and to indicate those constitutional and commercial problems which often serve as the mainsprings of political action.

The difficulties that beset any attempt to write

coherently on Greek history may be seen by a comparison with the history of Rome. There the issues are clear, the development continuous. Rome is a single city, gradually increasing her sway till she rules first Italy, then the whole of the Western world ; her constitution begins with the patriarchal principle —the father of the family ruling his clan with the advice of his council ; when the clans combine to form a state, this principle is extended to form the basis of the constitution—the King and his Senate rule the state ; the internal history of Rome is largely concerned with constitutional modifications to suit the circumstances as they arise, until finally, under stress of its own conquests, the city-state breaks down, and monarchy takes its place. But no such simple continuity must be looked for in the history of Greece ; cities rise and decline, new states come to the front, and this process continues right up to the time when Greece is absorbed in the Roman Empire. Almost every city forms a separate state in itself, of greater or less importance, and the history of Greece is largely a history of the struggles of these states with one another ; so the issues are not clear, development is not continuous : rather is there a series of developments, and each of the larger states —Athens, Sparta, Corinth, Thebes—might well have a volume to itself.

The conflicts between Greek and Greek are obvious, and lie on the surface of their history. The bonds that united them are none the less real because they are not so apparent : had they not been strong, the Greeks could not have created so distinct a civilisation, dependent not upon one or two states for its greatness, but upon many. The division into Greek and " barbarian," or non-Greek, is a very real one, and was recognised as such by the Greeks themselves ;

they realised that they came from the same stock. Their early constitutions were of the same " Aryan " type, though they developed along somewhat different lines ; the speech of one branch differed from that of another no more than the dialect of Yorkshire differs from that of Somerset ; their religion had a common source, and throughout their history they had common centres of worship, such as Delphi, and common religious festivals, such as that of the Olympic games.

But it is with their conflicts that we shall chiefly have to deal. Throughout Greek history there is a succession of these, and if we knew more of the early history of the Greeks there would no doubt be still more to record. The primitive historian deals chiefly, if not entirely, with wars, sometimes leaving even the causes undefined : it is not till much later that the " philosophic " historian comes to deal with the motives of political actions, with constitutional history as such, with the state of society at various times, and all those matters which have now come to be regarded as indispensable to a complete history of a nation. The early history of most nations is therefore confined to bare facts of doubtful authenticity, and inferences from survivals and from archæological discoveries take the place of authentic records. Particularly is this so in the case of Greece, whose early history is irrecoverable with any completeness : where the fact itself is often doubtful, and only the bare outlines can be traced : and where the accepted conclusions of one year may be overthrown by the discoveries of the next.

These conflicts, however, may usually be traced to one or more of three main causes, that run like a thread through Greek history. First comes commercial antagonism, due largely of course to geographical considerations; this will be referred to more particularly in the next chapter. Secondly, there are racial differences, of which the antagonism of Dorian and Ionian is the chief, never clearly defined, but constantly recurring; later we find Bœotian clashing with Dorian, Achæan with Ætolian. Thirdly, there are constitutional differences, prominent chiefly in the fifth century—the antagonism of oligarchy and democracy. These three threads combine to give some sort of unity to Greek history—a unity of conflict—in the Peloponnesian War, while at two great epochs all differences are set aside as the result of external pressure; at the time of the Persian wars, and again under the Macedonian domination, it is almost possible to speak of the Greek nation as a whole.

Naturally a succession of struggles brought a corresponding development of the art of war. In this matter Sparta took a long lead, for war was the whole business of a Spartan from the earliest times, while the other states relied on their "militia." After the Persian wars Athens developed a professional fleet, and so became by far the strongest naval power in the Greek world. Continued fighting, combined with the increase of wealth and capacity to pay soldiers, led at the beginning of the fourth century to the rise of a class of professional soldiers, and the supremacy of Sparta was doomed. Finally, the ideas of Epaminondas, developed by Macedon, led to the famous Macedonian phalanx, the engine by which Alexander the Great was enabled to conquer Persia.

So much, then, and only so much, common ground is there to work upon. The constitutional and territorial development of individual states is, however, more clearly defined, and their relations one to another are easier of description; with these we shall chiefly be concerned. It remains briefly to describe the settlement of the Greeks, and to indicate the lines upon which development is to be expected, and the order in which the various parts of the Greek world attained prominence.

The Greeks were a branch of the great family from which all the European nations are descended, and shared the pastoral habits of their Italian, Celtic, and Teuton kindred. They must have been the first to descend from the northern grass-lands to the Mediterranean, where they displaced an old and advanced Ægean civilisation, of which very important remains are at present being excavated, especially in Crete. The family or clan was the unit, both politically and socially, and survived sufficiently into historic times to enable us to realise that their early life must have been similar to that of Abraham— the typical pastoral community; their early constitutions, to use a very dignified term, would no doubt show a fairly close parallel to that of Rome, or of England in Anglo-Saxon times; this is certainly so in the case of Athens, and in a less degree in the case of Sparta, the only two states of whose constitutions we have any real record. The association of clans form a state to which the king stands in the same relation as the head of a clan does to its members; these heads of clans form the king's council, and there is an assembly of all members of the state, with little influence at first. This is the state of things which may be inferred from Homer, and to which inference from institutions that survived into historic times would lead us.

The change in the conditions of life that resulted from the southward migrations of the Greeks—a change from pastoral to agricultural and commercial life—naturally brought changes in their constitutions; and these changes resulted in at least an equal degree from geographical considerations, which largely helped to decide their way of life. The great majority of the Greek states were city-states—a strip of agricultural land, and a walled town as a centre of defence and of government. It is an unfortunate fact that the two states of which we know most, Athens and Sparta, were not really city-states, but approximated more to the modern idea of a state, with one important exception in the case of Athens; there, as in Miletus, Corinth, and other regular city-states, all citizens took an immediate part in the affairs of the state, and exercised such direct personal influence as they were capable of; and this is the chief distinction between Greek politics and our modern system of representative government.

The character of the country is especially favourable to the formation of small independent communities; a study of the map will show that it is extremely rugged, broken up by a succession of mountain-chains, with no plains of any extent save that of Thessaly—a collection of states that stands apart from the main current of Greek history—and the marshy Bœotia. There are no navigable rivers, and many of the streams are mountain-torrents, almost dry in the summer. The passes are difficult to force, and defensive warfare is easy. This does not prevent a continuous attempt on the part of the larger states to absorb the smaller, to go beyond the limitations of the city-state—an attempt that their unconquerable love of freedom led the Greeks to resist by every means in their power, to the extent of allying with, or even submitting to, the barbarian.

The small size of the states had important results,

both economically and politically. Development in every way was rapid; the small community soon ceased to be self-sufficing, trade became necessary, the surplus population was drafted off into colonies, manufactures increased, and means of communication were opened up with foreign countries. The simple patriarchal constitution no longer sufficed; the more necessary the bulk of the people became to the state, the more insistently they claimed a share in the government, and constitutional development proceeded with a rapidity far different to the slow growth of centuries in England. Politics were violent, as will easily be understood when we take into account the small numbers of the citizens, and the direct personal influence that prominent men must have exercised. Revolutions occurred not seldom; the best that a defeated party might hope for would be exile, and bloodshed was not infrequent. Home politics were often the determining factor in foreign policy; oligarchy would ally with oligarchy, democracy with democracy, and a change of government at home might mean a revision of all alliances abroad.

In these conditions it is not surprising to find the personal element prominent throughout, both for good and for evil; indeed, a study of Greek history from this standpoint would act as a useful corrective to the modern view that history is governed by immutable laws, and that the individual counts for nothing. To Themistocles it was given to change the history of a nation, to Alexander to change the history of the world.

The Greeks were divided into three great families, Ionian, Dorian, and Æolian. In historic times the Ionians occupied, in Greece proper, only Attica and Eubœa, and most of the islands that lay between these and Asia Minor—the Cyclades, with their centre at Delos, the island sacred to Apollo. The Dorians held all the east and south of the Peloponnese (the district south of the Corinthian Gulf), including Megara, Corinth, Sicyon, Argolis, Laconia, and Messenia ; Dorian also were Crete, Ægina, and the southern fringe of the Cyclades. The rest of the Peloponnese—Elis, Arcadia, Achaia—all Central Greece, from Bœotia in the east to Acarnania in the west, and Thessaly in the north, counted as " Æolian " ; this may be merely a convenient name to distinguish from the Ionians and Dorians all Greeks of different or " varied " race. Epirus counted as barbarian, and lay outside the current of Greek history, as did Macedonia for many centuries. The Æolians of Central Greece contain only one state, Thebes, of first-rate importance, while in the Peloponnese Achaia only rises into prominence in much later times, and Elis and Arcadia are chiefly of importance in connection with the rivalry of Sparta and Argos.

It is with the Ionians and Dorians that we shall principally be concerned at first. The Ionians were an energetic, inventive, and versatile race, good traders, good colonisers, always fond of " some new thing " ; and to them, and in especial to Athens, we owe most of what remains to us of Greek art and literature. The Dorians were slower to move, more conservative, more persevering ; equally good traders and colonisers, but without the daring enterprise that characterised the Ionians.

There are many problems connected with the settlements of the Greeks which it would be unprofitable to discuss. It is certain that the Dorians were the last to settle ; they came probably down the slopes of Mount Pindus, and then, by way of the Malian

(2,016)

Gulf, by sea to the Peloponnese, where they gradually conquered the regions which they held in historic times. They fall into two groups—the Argive, which includes Corinth, Sicyon, Phlius, &c., and the Spartan, which includes Crete and Messenia; the Spartan group had a distinct dialect and entirely different institutions, and the only things common to the two groups are the name Dorian, some similarity of dialect, and the cult of Apollo Carneius. The Spartans, we know, made no attempt to assimilate the conquered races; the Argives may have done so, and this would partially account for their more rapid development.

The Dorian invasion had one important result to the rest of Greece : tradition would make it the sole cause of the great migrations to the west coast of Asia Minor. This is, to say the least, improbable ; the progress made by the year 600, when Ionia was far in advance of Greece in all the essentials of civilisation, points to an earlier beginning for these settlements ; but reinforcements received from those who fled from the Dorians no doubt contributed largely to their early prosperity.

Of these settlements the Ionic were by far the most important ; they extended along the coast of Lydia and Caria, from Phocæa in the north to a point south of Miletus ; these two were important towns, especially the latter, and Ephesus, Colophon, and the islands of Chios and Samos were the other chief settlements. Athens claimed to be the metropolis or mother city of Ionia—a claim that cannot be substantiated ; her connection with Miletus was certainly intimate, but even Miletus cannot be regarded as an Athenian colony. In some of these cities, notably Ephesus, the Greeks must have coalesced with the Asiatic population : the famous " Diana of the Ephesians " (Acts xix. 24 foll.) was certainly an Oriental goddess.

The Æolians in the north were unimportant, except, perhaps, those of the island of Lesbos ; Smyrna, their chief mainland settlement, was detached by Ionia, and became a great trading station. The Dorian settlements, south of Ionia, came later, and were also unimportant ; they belong to the Argive group. Rhodes was the chief, but attained no prominence till much later. Halicarnassus was unimportant till it was Ionicised.

Thus when the historic period begins, we find the Greeks settled round the Ægean Sea, which was in effect a Greek lake, and did not, as now, divide East from West. The Greek world was to extend from Cyprus and the Crimea to Africa, Sicily, and the south of France ; but the Ægean is its heart, and it is there that its destinies are chiefly decided.

The first part of it to rise to prominence, under the influence of Asiatic civilisation, is Ionia ; but of Ionian greatness few records remain. Some brief notice of the chief cities will be given in the next chapter, when trade and colonisation are dealt with ; but it must not be forgotten that the Ionians were by 600 B.C. far in advance of Greece. Poetry had its home there—Homer was probably a Chian ; philosophy and art derived their origin from Ionian contact with the East ; and maritime enterprise was largely Ionic. Miletus was strong enough to treat with the Lydian kings, and even with Persia, on equal terms.

Crushed partly by Lydia and entirely by Persia, the Greeks of Asia declined, and the centre of power and influence in the Greek world shifts to Greece proper, where the great states found their power in time to deal successfully with the great Persian invasion. Sparta and Athens will chiefly claim our attention as the leading states in the fifth century, which ends with the fall of Athens ; then come the predominance of Thebes and the fall of Sparta. Worn out by their strife, the states of Greece proper fall a comparatively easy prey to Macedon, which, under Alexander, was destined to extend the Greek world much further East than ever before, and to give it a temporary unity ; but after his death his empire split up. Macedon resumes the position of a semi-alien power, and in Greece proper the exhaustion of Athens, Sparta, and Thebes leads to the rise of hitherto unimportant elements—the Achæan and Ætolian Leagues. Through the centuries the Greeks of the West—Sicily and South Italy—pursue their own course, always an integral part of the Greek world, but largely detached as regards politics. Finally, all these elements are absorbed by the conquering power of Rome, under whom Greek civilisation continued to be predominant over the whole of the eastern half of the Mediterranean.

II.—GREECE TO 500 B.C.

A.—EARLY DEVELOPMENT : TRADE AND COLONISATION.

OBSCURE traditions and legends, often manufactured to subserve political purposes, are all that remain to us of the history of the earliest times. As we advance, certain facts emerge which make it possible to give a broad outline of the history of some at any rate of the Greek states ; but we have no certain date before the middle of the sixth century, and problems, interesting but almost insoluble, abound— shifting perils through which it is hard to steer a safe course. The earliest extant historian, Herodotus, wrote in the middle of the fifth century, and his work is based upon oral tradition ; he was uncritical, his chronology is uncertain, and the motives he gives are often absurd, and coloured by the prejudices of his informants : while nominally writing a history of the relations of the Greeks with Lydia and Persia, he incorporated numerous stories relating to earlier times, and these are in many cases the only record that remains.

By 500 B.C. the constitutions of most of the states have passed through the period of transition, and have acquired the complexion that is to characterise them throughout the more definitely "historic" period. The old monarchial constitution—king, council, and assembly—has given way gradually as the result of changed conditions of life. Sparta alone in historic times had a kingly constitution. Of the normal development in its early stages Athens may perhaps be taken as a typical example, and will be discussed later in this chapter. Naturally, all the states did not develop quite on the same lines, but by 500 B.C. we find two types of constitution— oligarchy, the rule of the few, the principal men of the state, be it agricultural or commercial; and democracy, the rule of the whole people, destined to reach its height in the Athens of the fifth and fourth centuries.

Here it may be remarked that the condition of Greece as described by Homer does not concern us; logically, at any rate, it is anterior to the Dorian invasion and the settlements in Asia Minor, with which our history begins.

A simple statement of complex matters must suffice. The city-state settled into the form in which we know it in two ways, dependent one upon the other—partly by definite constitutional changes and partly by colonisation, which was usually a help to the aristocratic or oligarchic form of government. In some cases there is what is known as a synœcism —the formation of scattered agricultural villages into a city, with the consequent centralisation of government and its development from the simple patriarchal form to one more suited to the changing needs of the city.

The eighth and seventh centuries are the great colonising era. Colonies can be assigned to three causes, commercial, economic, and political. The small size of most of the states rendered trade necessary at an early stage—they could not be self-sufficing for long; and as many of the lands with which they traded were uncivilised, factories were established that developed into colonies. Economically, they served to draw off the surplus population of a city whose borders had become too strait for it ; and they were useful politically in providing an outlet for the energy of adventurous spirits who were discontented at home, and whose discontent was liable to take the form of political agitation. The development of these colonies was often very different from that of their mother-city or metropolis, and the tie that connected them—a religious tie—was not always very close.

The chief areas where colonies were planted were —in the north, the shores of the Black Sea, the Propontis, and Thrace ; in the west, the South of Italy, which became so Hellenised as to be called Magna Græcia, and Sicily. Miletus was the chief founder of colonies in the Black Sea ; over eighty factories are attributed to her, and these included several of the ports of modern Russia, and in the south Sinope and Trapezus (Trebizond, the seat of an Empire in the Middle Ages) ; to Megara, north of the Isthmus of Corinth, is ascribed the most famous of all—Byzantium (Constantinople), the gate of the Black Sea. Other famous colonies were Sestos and Abydos, opposite one another on the Hellespont, and in the Propontis Cyzicus.

In the North Ægean, Chalcis in Eubœa, with its neighbour Eretria, was the chief colonising city ; indeed, the three-pronged promontory of Chalcidice takes its name from Chalcis. The most important city in that district, Potidæa, was however a Corinthian colony. In the south the one great colony was Cyrene, a Dorian foundation famous for horses.

In the west the colonies fall naturally into three groups—Dorian, Chalcidic or Ionian, and Achæan.

The most important cities in Sicily were Dorian : Syracuse, destined to lead Greek Sicily against Carthage, was a daughter of Corinth, a city which had great interests and influence in the West ; and the four cities on the south coast, Camarina, Gela, Acragas (Agrigentum), and Selinus were all Dorian colonies. Later, Zancle, an Ionian colony, was taken by Dorians and renamed Messana : it gave its name to the straits between Sicily and Italy. The one great Dorian colony in Italy was Taras (Tarentum), the only colony founded by Sparta ; its foundation was due to political unrest.

Of the Ionian cities, Cyme or Cumæ, on the bay of Naples, was the oldest Greek colony in the west ; from it was founded Neapolis (Naples), close to it. To secure the straits between Sicily and Italy, Zancle and Rhegium were founded on either side, and from Zancle, before it was Dorized, came Himera, the only important Greek city on the north of Sicily. Naxos, Catana, and Leontini were founded on the west of Sicily, and Siris in the Tarentine Gulf had some early importance. Most of these owed their origin, in part at any rate, to Chalcis in Eubœa.

The Achæan colonies occupied most of the sea-board from Metapontum in the Tarentine Gulf to Poseidonia, south of Cumæ ; Sybaris, famous for luxury, and Croton were the chief ; the former extended its power across the " instep " of Italy, and Croton followed a similar course further south. They were as much agricultural as commercial settlements.

To secure the westward route Corinth colonised the island of Corcyra (Corfu).

Trade in the Ægean was mainly in the hands of the Phœnicians from 1000–800 B.C., and perhaps later. The influence of this people has been much exaggerated; their chief gift to the Greeks was the alphabet. When the Greeks began to trade for themselves, the Phœnicians, who were traders and not colonisers, seem to have retired, and gradually the Greeks not only ousted them from home waters, but became their rivals abroad. Our knowledge of Greek trade—a very interesting subject—is necessarily limited, especially in earlier times; no Greek historian was an economist, and scattered references in Herodotus to the " friendships " and wars, otherwise unaccountable, of distant cities, together with the remains of pottery, &c., form our chief evidence.

In the first half of the seventh century there are evidences of two trade leagues with wide connections. One, which we shall call the Chalcidian, extended its operations from Salamis in Cyprus to Sicily and Italy; working westward from Cyprus, we find Cyrene in Africa, and Cnidus in South-West Asia Minor connected; probably Crete, certainly Thera north of Crete. Then we come to the more important members—Samos, and probably Ephesus, well placed for trade with the Mæander valley; Chalcis in Eubœa : Corinth, perhaps the centre of the league. Corcyra, a colony of Corinth, was well placed on the westward route, but relations were soon strained, for tradition dates the first naval battle between Greek and Greek—Corinth against Corcyra—to 664 B.C. In the west, Tarentum : Croton and its dependencies : the Chalcidian colonies of Rhegium and Zancle, commanding the sea route to Central Italy, and the Chalcidian Cyme : and Syracuse, closely allied with Corinth, complete the known list of what must have been a widespread system.

The other league, called Eretrian, from the near neighbour of Chalcis, was equally wide, and its operations ranged from the Black Sea to Etruria. Miletus is the pivot in the east and north, with its far-reaching colonies in the Black Sea, connecting with the caravan trade to the Baltic, and its command of the Mæander valley, where before 500 B.C. it always out-distanced Ephesus ; Chios was the ally of Miletus, as Samos was the enemy. Siphnos, in the Ægean, and probably Andros, lead to Eretria, Athens, Ægina : in the Peloponnese Argos, some towns in Arcadia and Elis, and Sicyon : and some towns of Thessaly. In the west Sybaris, the wealthiest of Greek cities, was the centre ; the route would go overland—the straits being guarded by the Chalcidian League—to the dependencies of Sybaris and thence to Etruria.

We may suppose that the Chalcidian League was stronger by sea, and that the Eretrian coasted, and went by land where possible—*e.g.* across the Peloponnese and South Italy ; though indeed the Greek mariner, especially in the treacherous Ægean, seldom ventured out of sight of land with his small ships. There were no doubt many other places connected with one or the other of these leagues ; and it must not be supposed that these alliances were constant. The alliance of Corinth and Samos, for example, was one of oligarchy with oligarchy ; when Corinth is under a tyrant, we find him allied with the tyrant of Miletus. Some idea, however, will have been gained as to how the raw material—grain, cattle, and fish from the Black Sea, flax from Colchis, metal from Pontus and Cyprus, wool from Phrygia, and so forth —found its way to Greek manufactories, and where Milesian woollen goods, Tarentine fabrics, pottery from Etruria, Athens, Cnidus, Corinth, found a market.

Once at least we find the leagues in collision—

when Chalcis and Eretria fought for the Lelantine Plain, on which they stood, about 700 B.C., and "all Hellas took part on one side or the other ": Eretria was beaten, and partially crippled. This struggle was the most universal of any in the Greek world before the Peloponnesian War.

The connection of the Asiatic Greeks with Lydia and Egypt deserves some mention. About 670 B.C. a new and vigorous dynasty came to the throne of Lydia, and at first strove to reduce the Greek cities on its coast. Colophon and Priene fell, and Miletus and Smyrna were attacked but resisted. There was never any unity amongst the Ionians; commercial rivalry prevented that. Lydia, however, made peace, as its commercial policy demanded; it was a rich country, and the invention of coins is ascribed to it, showing considerable commercial prosperity; Crœsus, the last king of Lydia, is proverbial for his wealth. For two reigns or more the Lydians were fully occupied with the Cimmerians, a nomad tribe which came from the North and for a time overran Asia Minor; then Alyattes, a great Lydian king, expelled them, took Phrygia and Caria, extended his dominions to the Halys, and warred against the Medes. The wealthy Greek cities always attracted the Lydian kings. Alyattes took and destroyed Smyrna (before 600 B.C.), and attacked Miletus, which, as usual, proved strong enough to defend itself, and made a treaty in the end. This lasted during the reign of Crœsus (560–546 B.C.), whose one exploit was the capture of Ephesus; his reign ended with his defeat by Cyrus of Persia, who overran Lydia and reduced all the Greek cities except Miletus, whose strength is again shown by the willingness of the conqueror to make a treaty. This time the islands near the coast submitted; Cyprus and the Hellespontine region also fell. The subsequent relations of the Asiatic Greeks to Persia, and the Ionic Revolt, form a natural prologue to the Persian wars.

There are two main trade routes from the coast to the interior of Asia Minor—the Mæander and Hermus valleys. Miletus commanded the former, and with its population both of merchants and manufacturers—sometimes at strife with one another —was always a centre of trade in the Ægean : from 700 to 500 B.C. it was undoubtedly the greatest of the Ionic cities. Smyrna commanded the Hermus valley, and was the great town of the North, till broken up by Alyattes ; hence the rise of Phocæa, unimportant both before and after the Lydian dynasty. The Phocæans showed amazing enterprise : the modern towns of Marseilles, Nice, and Monaco were their colonies ; they penetrated to Tartessus in Spain (the Tarshish of the Bible), beyond the Straits of Gibraltar. When threatened by Persia, they migrated and tried to found a colony in Corsica ; this roused the Etruscans and Carthaginians, who combined against them. The Phocæans won a naval battle, but lost heavily in ships and men, and eventually settled in Elea in South Italy. Miletus benefited by their destruction. The great wealth of Ephesus, as we shall see, followed upon the Ionic Revolt.

Greek relations with Egypt began about the middle of the seventh century. Ionians ('' bronze men from the sea '') helped to liberate Egypt from the Assyrian yoke ; Ionian and Carian mercenaries helped Pharaoh Neco to defeat Josiah, king of Judah, at Megiddo. Miletus, Samos, and Ægina were the three chief cities trading with Egypt, and possessed separate temples, used as banking-houses, at the Greek '' colony '' of Naucratis at the mouth of the Nile. The other trading communities had a common temple.

B.—ARGOS, SPARTA, AND THE PELOPONNESE.

All tradition points to the early predominance of Argos in the Peloponnese ; but of the nature and extent of her influence little is known. In later times Argos was always the enemy of Sparta, and sometimes a serious rival for the hegemony, or leadership of the Peloponnese. Certainly Argos developed earlier than Sparta, possibly owing to some assimilation of the peoples conquered at the time of the Dorian Invasion ; her early constitution was kingly, but of its modifications nothing is known. The evidence we have points to early suzerainty over Corinth, Sicyon, Phlius, Cleonæ, and Ægina, and alliance with, if not some form of lordship over, Arcadia and Pisa. Her greatest king, Pheidon, whose date is a matter of controversy, but was probably about 750 B.C., introduced weights and measures into the Peloponnese, and helped Pisa to celebrate the Olympic games, of which Elis claimed the presidency. The introduction of weights and measures—this scale was known as the Æginetan, and was of Phœnician origin—shows Argos as an important trading power.

Of early Sparta we can gather a little more, though there are many problems whose solution is doubtful. Sparta stood upon excellent agricultural land, in the valley of the Eurotas, rather confined by mountains, and difficult of egress on every side. Sparta never attempted to assimilate the conquered population, and this gave the state a peculiarity that rendered it unique. The pure Spartans had beneath them Periœci, subordinate, but not without rights ; beneath these were the Helots, serfs, largely outnumbering both. Their origin is obscure ; by the

time of Thucydides (400 B.C.) all counted as Dorians.
The Helots required constant watching, and the
Spartans lived, as it were, beside a volcano—the
fear of a Helot rising. This accounts largely for
their whole organisation ; they became an exclusive
warrior caste, organised for war alone, with a state-
regulated system, which directed their whole life.
So, as a nation of professional soldiers, they played
a great part in Greek history ; but an account of
Greek civilisation might leave them out of account,
except for their constitution.

That, no doubt, developed from the primitive
system—king, council (called at Sparta Gerousia),
and assembly (Apella) ; later the Ephors, oligarchic
officials, became powerful, and were a check on the
kings. The great peculiarity at Sparta was that
there were two kings—possibly the result of a synœcism of two communities on equal terms. A rather
late tradition assigns the whole constitution to the
mythical Lycurgus—a name which stands, if for
anything, for the organisation of the Spartan system
of life. Under this constitution the Spartans proved
themselves capable of a firmer policy and more
sustained effort than any other Greek state.

There is no reason to doubt that the unanimity
on which their very existence depended characterised
Spartan policy from the outset, and they began with
a policy of conquest. After securing the Eurotas
valley from the sea to the borders of Arcadia, they
attacked their Dorian kinsmen in the fertile land of
Messenia. The first Messenian War, in the later half
of the eighth century, ended in Spartan success ;
the Messenians were reduced to the condition of
Helots. Political unrest, of obscure origin, led about
this time to the foundation of the only Spartan
colony, Tarentum.

Sparta was now a serious rival to Argos, and in 669 B.C. Argos won a great victory at Hysiæ : possibly Sparta had already seized the Argive district of Cynuria on the east of Laconia. This defeat did not alter Spartan determination, and the Second Messenian War (about 650–620 B.C.) may be regarded as an effort on the part of Argos to maintain her waning power in the Peloponnese. In this war, revolted Messenia is supported by Argos, Pisatis, and Arcadia ; Sparta has the help of Elis. Sparta won in the end ; Messenia, Cynuria, and (later) Thyreatis were secured, and Sparta was master of the southern Peloponnese from sea to sea. Elis secured Pisatis and Triphylia —the latter geographically and ethnically Arcadian.

Then came a change. Two of the three roads to the north were held by Argos and Tegea ; the latter was first attacked, but the Spartans were defeated— a defeat which changed their whole policy. Tegea was eventually overcome, but admitted to alliance (*circa* 560 B.C.), and thenceforth Sparta, realising perhaps that the numbers of her citizens were insufficient for a wide scheme of conquest, and naturally disinclined to admit the lower orders to equal rights, aimed not at conquest, but at the hegemony of Greece. It is perhaps at this time that the Ephors obtained power equal, if not superior, to that of the kings.

This policy had great results : by 500 B.C. Sparta was allied with all the Peloponnese except Argos and Achaia, and beyond the Isthmus with Megara and Ægina ; at one time with Athens, at another with Thebes and Chalcis. The alliances with the rest of Arcadia, Corinth, and Ægina may be assigned to the years 550–520 B.C. ; the others to the reign of Cleomenes, about 520–488 B.C. This great king directed Spartan policy for thirty years, and had a great reputation throughout the Greek world; his whole aim was the extension of Spartan influence, and the overthrow of any power that threatened to rival Sparta—this indeed is the keynote of Spartan policy for the next 150 years. Hence Spartan antagonism to tyrannies, and the suppression of those of Sicyon and Athens; hence too the willing admission of first Athens, then Thebes and Chalcis, to the Peloponnesian League.

But the expansion of Spartan power had been too rapid; in his second expedition (506 B.C.) against Athens, which will be dealt with later, the Peloponnesian section of the League, headed by Corinth, deserted Cleomenes, and his king-colleague Demaratus played him false; so he deserts his extra-Peloponnesian allies, and devotes his time to consolidating Spartan power within the Isthmus. For twelve years Sparta is quiescent, refusing those appeals to help in distant expeditions, which were naturally made to the chief state of Greece; the defection of Corinth has evidently caused Argos once more to raise her head, and Cleomenes is preparing for the great battle which in 495 B.C.—to give the most probable date—crushed Argos and reasserted Spartan supremacy. This is a turning-point in Greek history; it was the most decisive victory of Greek over Greek till the Peloponnesian War. Corinth now gives no opposition, Athens seeks alliance, Ægina yields, and Sparta attains a position of undisputed hegemony in Greece, but for which there could have been no resistance to Persia.

One point needs notice; the action of Corinth was partly due to her having trade interests in common with Athens as against Ægina, but also to a desire for balance of power, a political principle peculiarly adapted to her geographical position—it did not suit Corinth that Sparta should be supreme on both sides of the Isthmus.

C.—The Tyrannis.

The word *tyrant* implies simply an unconstitutional ruler, without any reference to the goodness or badness of his rule.   Tyranny must first have sprung up amongst the Asiatic Greeks, a result of their proximity to the despotism of the East ; and a wave of tyranny came over from Asia between 650 and 550 B.C., affecting Corinth, Sicyon, Epidaurus, Megara, Athens ; this extends to the West between 520 and 460 B.C. But to speak of an " Age of the tyrants " because of the experience of these few cities is to forget the far greater number which never were under a tyrant. The expression seems also to give to the various tyrannies a unity which they were far from possessing, and this false impression has been aggravated by Greek political philosophy, which speaks of tyranny as the transition stage between oligarchy and democracy ; but there is only one instance—Athens— where this was certainly the case.   The tyrant was really a politician who succeeded in turning political discontent to his own uses, and thereby became master of the state ; and our brief notices of the various tyrannies will only serve to show the infinite diversity of conditions that prevailed in the Greek states.

Of the tyrannies of Asiatic Greece little is known. Thrasybulus of Miletus (*circa* 600 B.C.) formed a connecting link between Lydia and Corinth.   In Samos Polycrates took advantage of Persian weakness at sea to found a tyranny, and established a reign of terror in the Ægean in the latter part of the sixth century ; he seems to have been little more than a strong pirate, and is an example of the worse class of tyrant. His cupidity eventually brought him into the hands of the Persians, and he was put to death. The numerous tyrants who acted as Persian governors in Ionia and Cyprus after the Persian conquest are merely the expression of subjection to the " Great King " of Persia—a despot naturally ruled by means of subordinate despots.

The Corinthian is the most important of the earlier tyrannies in Greece itself. Corinth was ruled by a Dorian clan, the Bacchiadæ ; Cypselus, a Bacchiad, took advantage of the discontent of the rest of the Dorians of Corinth to seize the government in their interest, about 657 B.C. ; he was succeeded by his son Periander. The tyranny hardly survived the latter, and in 583 Corinth reverted to an oligarchic form of government. The Corinthian tyrants showed the natural predilection for foreign and dynastic alliances which marks all tyrannies ; they had relations with Lydia and Egypt, and with other tyrants at Miletus and Epidaurus ; the Greeks, for the most part, did not intermarry with other Greek states, so the frequency with which tyrants intermarried with the families of other tyrants—and occasionally with " barbarians "—is the more remarkable. Besides these connections, Periander considerably increased the direct power of Corinth, and by reducing Corcyra to obedience, and making Apollonia, Ambracia, and Epidamnus subject, he secured a free route for Corinthian trade to the West ; his policy shows a breadth of view that would be sought in vain from the commercial oligarchy of later times.

The tyranny at Sicyon had a different origin ; the non-Dorian population rose against its Dorian masters, and in 665 their leader, Orthagoras, became

tyrant. Cleisthenes was the most influential tyrant
of this line, and under him the Dorians were debased;
the old dependency upon Argos was ended, and the
tyranny lasted till 520 B.C., or later, when the Spartans
restored to the Dorian element its supremacy. The
tyranny of Cleisthenes is the only period at which
Sicyon possessed anything like first-class importance;
he was one of the generals in the Sacred War to support pilgrims to Delphi against piratical exactions,
and the good story of his daughter's wedding, as
told by Herodotus, shows that Sicyon had strong
allies.

Of other tyrannies, that of Theagenes of Megara
vaguely represented " the poor against the rich,"
and little is known of it. Peisistratus of Athens will
be noticed in the next section; it may here be said
that he owed his power to his championship of the
poorer farming class against the nobles. The Sicilian
tyrants who ruled at the time of the Persian Wars
are of great importance, and will be more fully dealt
with in Chapter VIII.; we may note that Gelo of
Syracuse was invited by the oligarchy to become
tyrant, and that in the fourth century Dionysius
founded his power by subverting a corrupt democracy.

The tyrants are an interesting personal study, and
this causes them to bulk rather largely in Herodotus,
especially those whom Nemesis overtook. Their
characteristics are those of most absolute rulers, and
naturally some were better and wiser than others;
the best of them did much for their city, identifying
its interests with their own, and in one or two cases
pointed the way to its future greatness; the worst
gave the name of tyrant its modern meaning. Several of them were generous patrons of art, poetry,
and philosophy, and their " courts " became centres

of culture. Peisistratus and his sons at Athens,
Hiero and Dionysius at Syracuse, are notable in-
stances of this.

D.—ATHENS.

Athens is the one state of whose constitutional
development and politics we can form some broad
conception, though much is dark ; in most other
cases, when we hear of constitutional changes they
are usually violent, from oligarchy to democracy,
or vice versa, with no note of development ; but
Athens is remarkable for the peacefulness of its constitutional changes, though some of them were not
accomplished without bloodshed. In this gradual
development of the typical democracy we shall,
however, note the great influence, even in the later
stages, of the old families, of whom the chief are the
Alcmæonidæ, the Philaidæ, and the Peisistratidæ.
Members of all these families contracted alliances
with the tyrants of the Northern Peloponnese ; one
succeeded in establishing a tyranny at Athens,
another in Thrace, and when constitutional government was restored to Athens, and the Peisistratids
were expelled, the other two supported rival policies
and headed rival parties.

There are evidences of two elements in the population—an indigenous " Attic " and an immigrant
Ionic, united from early times ; the synœcism of
Attica, in this case the uniting of the inhabitants in
a common citizenship, is attributed to the hero
Theseus. The early development follows a natural
course : the king, with threefold power—pontifical,
judicial, military—the council of nobles, the assembly
of the people, are first found. Gradually the king
has his powers cut down, then ceases to exist ; his

place is taken by an oligarchy, wherein the *polemarch* has the military power, the *archon* the judicial ; offices are held at first for ten years, then for one, and by successive accretions of power the archon becomes the chief magistrate of the state ; thus the council of nobles, from which the archons were drawn, becomes the stronghold of a strict oligarchy, while popular institutions are yet unknown.

Unrest, both economic and political, showed itself in an abortive attempt to found a tyranny towards the close of the seventh century, and in Draco's codification of the laws ; judicial power was in the hands of the nobles, and the people were hitherto liable to arbitrary punishments. But the evil was too deep-seated for this to be effective ; war with Megara for the possession of Salamis increased the prevailing depression, and the time was ripe for Solon's legislation. His conquest of Salamis gave him great influence, and he was appealed to by all classes to mediate. The grievances of the people were chiefly economic, aggravated by the fact that they had no political powers. The land was in the hands of a few ; the tenant-farmers, if they failed to pay rent, were sold into slavery with their wives and children. Solon seems to have converted the tenant-farmers into peasant-proprietors, possibly to have cancelled all debts, and certainly to have prohibited borrowing upon the security of the debtor's person. To encourage Athens' growing trade with the Ægean and North-West, he changed the coinage from the Æginetan scale, used by her enemies Ægina and Megara, to the Euboic, used by Chalcis, Corinth, and the wider Greek world. His constitutional changes were parallel ; the citizens were divided into four classes according to wealth derived from land. The highest class alone was eligible for the higher offices ; the lowest was excluded from all. With privileges went duties, and the classes served as cavalry, heavy-armed and light-armed infantry, according to their income. All the people were given a share in the *ecclesia* (assembly) and the law-courts, with the right to elect magistrates and examine their accounts. The council (hereafter called the Areopagus) was deprived of its administrative functions, but retained the important duty of protector of the laws, and a second council (*Boulê*) was instituted, containing 100 members from each of the four old Ionic tribes, with the duty of preparing business for the ecclesia ; its powers seem to have been very limited before 510 B.C.

Solon's laws are the real foundation of the Athenian democracy ; but they were at first a failure. Anarchy followed ; both classes were discontented ; the poor had expected more advantages, the nobles less change. As wealth from land was necessary for high office, the mercantile classes were dissatisfied ; while many inhabitants of Attica were still excluded from citizenship. Hence we find three parties—that of the Plain (larger landholders or aristocrats) led by Miltiades the Philaid, and afterwards by Lycurgus ; the Coast (merchants—moderates) led by Megacles the Alcmæonid ; and the Hill, led by Peisistratus. The last class formed the germ of the future democratic party, and was made up partly of small farmers, partly of those who feared to lose the franchise if their opponents prevailed ; their leader, Peisistratus, succeeded in establishing himself as tyrant. Miltiades retired and founded a tyranny in the Thracian Chersonese. Peisistratus was driven out by a coalition of Lycurgus and Megacles, but married the latter's daughter, and returned ; a quarrel with Megacles again led to his expulsion, but he again returned, and ruled till his death. These leaders all seem to have acted entirely from selfish motives.

Peisistratus ruled well, and in accordance with Solon's laws ; to him and to Cleisthenes' subsequent legislation is to be attributed the economic stability of Athens in the fifth century ; certainly after his time the landholder is usually a peasant-proprietor. He established local courts in the country districts, organised the water supply, took measures to advance Athenian commerce, manufactures, and art, and formed alliances and created dependencies in many parts of the Greek world. He was allied by marriage with Argos, friendly with Sparta, Thessaly, Eretria, and Thebes ; further afield he was connected with Macedon and Lampsacus ; Thrace at the mouth of the Strymon, Sigeum (ruled by his son), and Naxos (ruled by a subordinate tyrant) seem to have been subject to him. Sigeum and the Thracian Chersonese commanded the corn-route from the Black Sea, and the settled conditions at Athens, combined with a strong foreign policy, greatly increased Athens' commercial power.

In 528 B.C. Peisistratus died, and was succeeded by his sons Hippias and Hipparchus, who continued their father's policy, and, like him, encouraged literature and art. The conspiracy of Harmodius and Aristogeiton, prompted by private grievances, resulted in the assassination of Hipparchus (514 B.C.), but Hippias escaped, and thereafter ruled more strictly. The Philaids had been treated with moderation by the Peisistratids, but the Alcmæonids, after the quarrel of Peisistratus and Megacles, had been in exile ; they were wealthy and ambitious, and after one attempt to turn out Hippias had failed, they prevailed with the Delphic oracle to persuade

Sparta to expel him ; this was done by Cleomenes in person, after a smaller expedition had failed, in 510 B.C.

Cleisthenes, the Alcmæonid leader, did not, however, reign supreme ; he was beaten in the oligarchic political clubs by Isagoras, who was elected archon for 508, whereupon, with the usual unscrupulousness of the Alcmæonids, he went over to the popular side and offered the franchise to the commons. Isagoras again called in Cleomenes, who expelled certain families from Athens, but the Boulê resisted him, and he was besieged in the Acropolis.   Eventually he was allowed to depart.   Cleisthenes returned, and carried his legislation.   As an astute party politician, he saw where Solon had failed, and proceeded to split up the old local factions.   He substituted ten new tribes for the old four, giving to each a group of demes—the existing small local divisions—from each district, and making the new tribes the centre of administration.   As each tribe contained members from each of the old centres of civil strife, the fact that they had to act together politically under the new system made the old strife impossible, and destroyed the local influence of the landlord class. A corresponding increase was made in the numbers of the Boulê, from 400 to 500—50 from each tribe. It seems that he also enrolled many in the new tribes who had been excluded from the old, thus increasing the number of citizens and of his own supporters. The four Ionic tribes remained, but only for religious purposes—their political importance passed away. One other law there is, that of ostracism, a peculiar system which was perhaps designed to prevent tyranny, but soon became an instrument of party politics.   A vote could be called for once a year, and if 6000 votes were polled, the man against whom the majority were cast was exiled for ten years. This measure practically deprived the aristocratic Areopagus of its guardianship of the constitution; the Boulê became the safeguard of the ecclesia, and the keystone of the constitution.

Cleisthenes' constitutional changes had eventually the result of setting up two parties at Athens on new lines, both supporters of the constitution, but with different policies; but this took time, and for some years the great families were still intriguing for their personal supremacy. There were two quarters from which aid might be looked for—Sparta and Persia. Hippias had gone to Sigeum, and was endeavouring to gain Persian help; Isagoras invoked Cleomenes' aid, and the expedition whose failure we have already noted (p. 31) was the result. Cleisthenes, to meet pressure from Sparta and her northern allies Thebes and Chalcis, applied to Persia, hoping to get aid at the price of merely nominal submission; thus Athens was the first state in Greece to " medise," *i.e.* to join the " Medes " or Persians, and this seems to have been Cleisthenes' undoing, for he disappears entirely from history. Athens succeeded in defeating both Thebes and Chalcis, but still feared intervention from Persia to restore Hippias, and sent a second embassy to the Persian governor at Sardis, apparently offering submission, provided that no demand was made for the restoration of Hippias : this embassy seems to have failed. It is at this point that the Ionic Revolt brings matters to a head.

The action of Thebes in regard to Athens needs some comment. The chief aim of Thebes was to organise an obligatory Bœotian League, headed by herself, and this dominates her policy. Sparta naturally did not desire to see a league of any importance north of the Isthmus, which might prevent the extension of the Peloponnesian League ; accordingly, in 519, Cleomenes had supported the town of Platæa in its resistance to Thebes, and had placed it under the protection of Athens. But when Athens rejected Cleomenes, he joined with Thebes, now and henceforth hostile to Athens. The relations of these three powers are determined entirely by political considerations ; hence, when Athens is again allied to Sparta we find Thebes on the side of Persia.

III.—THE PERSIAN WARS.

It was the destiny of the Greek race for many centuries to be the safeguard of the West, and at one glorious epoch to hold the East in fee ; most famous of all the struggles of East and West are the Persian wars, in which the Greeks beat back an invasion whose success must have destroyed Western civilisation and have set back progress for centuries. It would be pleasant to think of these wars as a united effort on the part of the Greeks against the barbarians, but this we cannot do ; treachery in Athens itself, the great protagonist in the strife, dissension in the Peloponnesian League, and actual sympathy with the Mede from states which hoped to advance their own power, prevent us. Fortunately the general course of the wars is clear, though many of Herodotus' details are obscure.

The Persians, a race akin to the Medes and not distinguished from them by the Greeks, within thirty years conquered or received submission from Media, Lydia, and Ionia, Babylonia, Phœnicia, and Egypt. After a brief pause for organisation, King Darius conquered part of Thrace, but farther advance westward had to be postponed owing to the Ionic Revolt. The cities of Asiatic Greece were ruled by tyrants subordinate to Persia, one of whom, Aristagoras of Miletus, received permission to lead a fleet against Naxos, and reduce it for the Persians ; he failed, and

feared punishment from Persia, so, resigning his
tyranny, proposed to the assembled fleet (of Asiatic
Greeks subject to Persia) to get rid of their tyrants,
whom they hated, and revolt. The fact that the
fleet was assembled, and that the tyrants could be
seized at once, made the opportunity too tempting
to resist; but the Greeks soon found their mistake.
Aristagoras proved a weak leader; there was no
spontaneity in the revolt, nor was it general throughout the Greek world; little help was obtained from
Greece proper—Sparta was preparing to crush Argos
(p. 30), while at Athens the balance of parties was
too even for more than nominal aid to be rendered,
and this was withdrawn at the first defeat; Eretria
sent a few ships. Against a land-power like Persia—
which moreover had the aid of the Phœnician fleet—
a " backing " of land was needed, or the cities could
be picked off one by one. Offensive tactics alone
had any chance of success; these were at first
adopted, and Sardis, the capital of Lydia, was taken,
with immediate good results in the support of Caria
and Cyprus; but the Greeks burned the town of
Sardis, and this alienated the Lydians, who refused
to join: thereafter operations were almost entirely
defensive. Most destructive of all, however, was the
lack of unanimity among the Ionians themselves,
caused by the geographical position and commercial
rivalries of the cities; no Dorians, and only Lesbos
of the Æolians, joined; the Hellespontine region
lay crushed after a previous revolt; Ephesus held
aloof to gain the inland trade of Miletus. In the
final struggle the old rivalry between Samos and
Miletus broke out again; the Samians deserted, and
Chios alone remained faithful to its old ally Miletus.
The Revolt may be dated 499–494 B.C.; the Persians
gradually reduced the revolted districts, and after

the reduction of Cyprus the fleet was ready to move against Miletus. The final battle, that of Lade, was fought off Miletus; the city was taken, and its prosperity passed to Ephesus. The islands were reduced in the next year.

Darius was now ready to advance; he had already, in his Scythian expedition, conquered part of Thrace, and now sent Mardonius west with an army and fleet. On his way the latter established democracies in the Greek cities of Asia in place of the tyrannies—a striking proof of Darius' broad-mindedness. The rest of Thrace, Thasos, and Macedon were reduced (492), but the fleet was wrecked, and Mardonius could not proceed. Then, after ineffective embassies demanding the submission of Sparta and Athens, comes (490) the expedition of Datis and Artaphrenes, whose primary object seems to have been the punishment of Athens and Eretria for their share in the Ionic Revolt. They sailed across the Ægean, took and sacked Eretria, and landed at Marathon, on the north of Attica.

Meanwhile at Athens the situation had changed more than once. After their tentative participation in the Revolt, the Athenians had withdrawn, and had even elected the Peisistratid leader archon, perhaps as evidence of their willingness to receive back Hippias. But by 491 the situation had changed again; the capture of Miletus had moved Athens deeply. Miltiades, the third tyrant of the Thracian Chersonese, had returned, and reasserted the influence of the Philaidæ: in all probability he was joined by Themistocles, archon in 493, and Athens once more relied on Sparta. Hence we may expect to find the Alcmæonids ready again to medise. Ægina, now the commercial rival of Athens, gave earth and water —signs of submission—to Persia, and Athens appealed to Sparta, now the unquestioned head of Greece after her defeat of Argos, for help. Hostages were taken from the island and given to Athens, so that the quiescence of Ægina was assured. The Athenian army had recently been reorganised, and was now in the hands of ten generals, one elected by each tribe ; their relation to the Polemarch at the time of Marathon is uncertain, but the chief credit for the ensuing victory must certainly be given to Miltiades, one of the generals, whose knowledge of Persian organisation and tactics must have been invaluable.

The most probable order of events (obscure in Herodotus) is as follows : The Persians landed at Marathon, apparently to draw the Athenian forces from Athens, that in their absence traitors—Peisistratids and Alcmæonids—might betray the city, as had happened at Eretria ; they cannot have expected the Athenians to fight on ground so well suited for Persian cavalry. Miltiades proposed and carried a motion in the ecclesia that the Athenians should go to meet the Persians ; they encamped above Marathon, waiting for Spartan help (which eventually came too late), as the Persians waited for a sign from the traitors. On the field of battle 1000 Platæans joined the Athenian forces, making 10,000 or 11,000 in all ; the Persians had from 40,000 to 60,000 men. The Persians decided to leave a containing force to hold Miltiades, and to send a detachment to capture Athens ; they waited, however, for the signal from the city, but the plotters were not ready, and at last the Persians anticipated the signal, and divided their forces, embarking part —including the cavalry, which would be useful on the plain of Athens—to move round by sea to the city. This division of the Persian forces compelled

Miltiades to act : fearing to be enveloped by the greater number of the Persians, he made his line of equal length with theirs by thinning out his centre ; the strong wings drove back the Persians, whom they allowed to fly, then turned and attacked the enemy's centre, which was having the better of the fight. The Persians were completely routed, and those who could fled to the ships ; the Persian dead numbered over 6000, the Athenian 192. The Persians pursued their plan of sailing round to Athens, encouraged by the traitors' signal—the flashing of a shield, attributed to the Alcmæonids ; but Miltiades returned direct to Athens by forced marches. The Persian demonstration in Athenian waters was thus rendered useless, and they departed across the Ægean. The moral result of this battle was enormous ; it was the first defeat of Persian Greek, and the *hoplite* (heavy-armed soldier) fully proved his value ; moreover, both tyranny and medism were now rendered impossible at Athens.

Persian preparations for their next invasion of Greece were on a grand scale, but when Darius had thus occupied two years, the revolt of Egypt delayed him ; he died in 485, and its subjugation was left to his son and successor, Xerxes, who was not ready to move against Greece till late in 481, so that the Greeks had more respite than they had expected. They did not, however, employ these years entirely in concerted preparation ; their inter-state rivalries continued as before, and one man alone, Themistocles the Athenian, perhaps the greatest statesman Greece ever produced, grasped the situation clearly and worked unceasingly with one great aim in view— to provide a permanent Athenian fleet large enough and strong enough to meet the Persians. His success in this determined the fate of Greece, and fitted

Athens for her future career of greatness. Before Marathon he had fortified the Peiræus, the port of Athens, by a wall ; he had no doubt the help of Miltiades, who, however, was soon removed from the scene. After Marathon he attacked Paros—a suitable outpost against a Persian expedition across the Ægean—but was wounded and failed ; on his return he was impeached by Xanthippus the Alc-mæonid, and condemned to pay a fine, but died of his wound : the fine was paid by his son Cimon. This incident strikingly illustrates the extreme personal responsibility of the executive in Greek states.

The result of the Parian expedition was the brief ascendancy of the Alcmæonids, but Themistocles' naval policy soon carried the day. Athens had already a flourishing commerce to protect, and he had, no doubt, the support of the merchant classes. One by one he secured the ostracism of his chief opponents: Hipparchus, leader of the Peisistratid party ; Megacles, official leader of the Alcmæonids ; Xanthippus, their practical leader; Aristides the Just, his political associate and ally. The war with Ægina, for the command of the Saronic Gulf, acted as an excuse, of which he made skilful use to advance his projects. Athens had refused to give back the Æginetan hostages after Marathon, but this had been counterbalanced by the Æginetan capture of an Athenian ship containing many prominent citizens ; presumably hostages were exchanged, and war was carried on in earnest. Athens had the support of Corinth, a trade rival of Ægina ; we shall find that Corinth's attitude to Athens was dictated by commercial, as her attitude to Sparta was dictated by political, considerations. The war was carried on with varying success, and was still undetermined when the invasion of Xerxes sank minor differences, and at Salamis Athens, Corinth, and Ægina are found fighting side by side. One notable constitutional change belongs to this period ; in 487, a law was passed that the archons should be chosen by lot, still from the higher classes, so that it was not a democratic device ; perhaps this measure was adopted to prevent faction in the state, which centred round the archonship. The chief result was that henceforth the generals—an elective office—became the executive of Athens ; this military executive lasted for 150 years.

Sparta also had her troubles. Cleomenes succeeded in deposing Demaratus, his fellow-king, who had twice balked his projects ; but the means he took to do so were doubtful, and his own personality was too strong for such a state as Sparta. He was banished, but showed his power by forming an Arcadian League, devoted to himself ; this secured his recall, but he soon died, and the mysterious circumstances of his death point to assassination. He had shown the essential weakness, by his organisation of Arcadia, of that Spartan hegemony of which he was the chief founder ; but the Spartans took measures that the kings, whose constant feuds discredited them, should henceforth be no more than the servants of the state. The direction of foreign policy passed to the Ephors. Their influence in the Peloponnese was, however, weakened ; Elis and Mantinea sent their contingents " too late " for the battle of Platæa.

In the spring of 480 Xerxes and his great armament moved from Sardis, crossed the Hellespont by a bridge of boats, and proceeded through Thrace and Macedon, with army and fleet in close conjunction. This co-ordination of the two services forms an integral part of Persian strategy, and its advantages are obvious ; but it had also disadvantages, as when in 492 Mardonius was unable to proceed farther than Macedon because his fleet was wrecked off Mount Athos, whose dangers on this occasion were circumvented by a canal. The numbers Herodotus gives are incredible—over 2,000,000 fighting men, and 500,000 to man the fleet ; adding a servant for each, he gets over 5,000,000, camp-followers to be added *ad lib.* If we reduce this to six army corps of 50,000 infantry and 10,000 cavalry each, we shall get nearer to probability : perhaps 330,000 in all, for the cavalry seem to have been halved, as being of less use in rugged Greece. The fleet numbered 1207 ships-of-war, in addition to transport vessels, &c. ; they chiefly came from Phœnicia, Egypt, Cyprus, Cilicia, and Asiatic Greece. The organisation of the expedition seems to have been excellent.

The Greeks, it will be seen, had to meet both army and fleet at once with inferior forces. On land they were handicapped by the necessity of leaving a garrison in the Peloponnese, for the Persians might send a squadron round ; moreover, the Helots were always ready to revolt, and from Argos could be expected at best an armed neutrality : and the Peloponnesians formed the most important part of the Greek land-forces. Hence the Peloponnesian policy of Sparta—to build a wall across the Isthmus and defend it, letting central Greece take its chance ; this suicidal policy was only defeated by Themistocles' insistence on the value of the Athenian fleet, and his threat to depart westwards and found a new Athens in Italy. In any case the army must act on the defensive against the superior Persian forces, and fortunately there were several points at which such defence was feasible—notably Tempe in North

Thessaly, Thermopylæ on the Malian Gulf, and the Isthmus. The function of the fleet was different ; it had some chance in offensive warfare, but only if the large Persian fleet was compelled to fight at a disadvantage in confined waters ; hence the army must check the Persian army, in conjunction with which the fleet has to act, at some point which will make it either fight in confined waters or lose touch with the land-forces. Such a point was Artemisium, off the north of Eubœa : the whole inner coast from Tempe to Marathon can be guarded by a fleet placed there, and a Greek blocking-force either at Tempe or Thermopylæ would achieve the object of making the Persian fleet fight at a disadvantage ; strategic-ally, it is a better position than Salamis, where the final naval battle was fought. The credit for Greek naval strategy must go to Themistocles.

A force of 10,000 men was sent to guard Tempe, but it proved that an outflanking movement through the mountains would present no difficulty to the Persians, and the Greeks retired : thus Thessaly was lost to them ; its princes had wished to medise, but the common people had not. Thermopylæ, on the southern frontier of Thessaly, is a better position ; there were two passes, one along the coast, a bare hundred yards wide, where Leonidas made his famous stand, the other up the Asopus gorge, ap-parently at this time defended by Trachis ; this was the usual pass into Central Greece. The Spartans took half measures, sending their King Leonidas with 300 Spartans ; his whole force amounted to 5000 men, enough to defy a frontal attack, and was perhaps sufficient if its object was merely to give the fleet a chance to strike a decisive blow, especially if we con-sider its precarious position if the fleet were defeated ; Persian troops could then be landed in the rear.

On the first two days the Persians made a merely nominal attack on Thermopylæ ; they had sent 200 ships round Eubœa, hoping to turn the position. The Greeks, it seems, met this by guarding the Euripus, the narrow channel between Eubœa and the mainland, with 53 ships. A storm arose and destroyed the Persian turning squadron off the rocky coast of Eubœa (400 ships were destroyed in all), and the 53 ships returned to Artemisium with the tidings. The Greeks had on the two preceding days attacked detachments of the Persian fleet with considerable success, and Themistocles' tactics were promising well ; the failure of the turning movement by sea led, however, to a general engagement, wherein the Greeks did no more than hold their own, but prevented any landing of the troops in the rear of Leonidas. On the fourth day the Greek fleet was compelled to retreat, owing to the failure of the land force at Thermopylæ ; the existence of another path was betrayed to the Persians, and a picked force under Hydarnes was sent to turn Leonidas' position. This path seems to have been guarded, but the Phocians, who held it, fled—to guard Delphi, they said ; but the attitude of the oracle was suspicious, and there can be little doubt that Delphi medised. Realising the position of affairs, Leonidas sent away his Peloponnesian troops, but himself remained with his 300 Spartans, supported by 700 Thespians and 400 Thebans (a patriotic minority from medising Bœotia), and gave the world its most famous example of how to die a noble death. His motives are not clear ; the fine tradition that a Spartan must never retreat seems to take its rise from this very action ; and it is quite possible that a stern fatalism led him to fulfil the oracle that either Sparta itself, or a king of Sparta, must fall before the Persian. When he saw himself surrounded, he advanced to meet the foe, and his little army, after heroic deeds, perished to a man. He did not die in vain ; his failure, more glorious than success, did much to inspire the Greeks with courage for the task that lay before them.

Central Greece now lay at the invaders' mercy. Bœotia received them willingly ; Phocis was devastated at the instance of its hereditary foes, the Thessalians ; Attica was overrun and Athens razed to the ground. The Athenians seem to have expected the Peloponnesian League to fight in Bœotia ; when disappointed, they conveyed their families to Ægina, Salamis, and Trœzen, and placed their trust in the fleet, to which, out of a total of 378 ships, they contributed 180 ; Corinth with 40, and Ægina with 30, approached nearest to this total. The confined waters that lay inside Salamis were admirably suited to Themistocles' tactics—the Persian numbers would actually be a hindrance, and the superior fighting capacity of the Greek marines would be an advantage at close quarters ; but he had the greatest difficulty in persuading his fellow-admirals not to retreat to the Isthmus, and finally had recourse to the desperate measure of sending a messenger to tell Xerxes that the Greeks were contemplating flight. Xerxes divided his forces, preferring the chance of a brilliant victory to the comparative certainty of success by surer methods, and sent the Egyptian contingent to block the western exit from the bay of Eleusis ; it would appear that the Corinthian squadron was detached to meet them. The battle took place at the eastern side of Salamis : the Athenians, on the Greek left, met the Phœnicians, whose ships, crowded into a narrow space, fouled each other. The details are obscure, but it seems that the Æginetans broke through on the right and completed the disorganisation of their enemies ; in the *mêlée* that followed the Greeks were completely victorious. Night fell, and when day dawned the Persian fleet had gone ; the Greeks pursued as far as Andros. Xerxes himself retired, escorted by one army corps, leaving Mardonius, the real leader of the expedition, to make preparations for the subjugation of the rest of Greece in the following year. The story of Xerxes' precipitate flight was no doubt exaggerated : the king of a vast empire was needed at the centre of affairs, and had no doubt little reason or inclination to spend the winter in Greece.

The battle of Salamis did not determine the fate of Greece. It decided that the Persians could no longer carry out the design of attacking the Peloponnese by sea and land conjointly ; but so long as Sparta refused to advance north of the Isthmus, it was open to the Persians to organise Northern and Central Greece, as a Persian province, while their fleet, though scattered, was still to be reckoned with.

Mardonius wintered in Thessaly ; realising the value of the Athenian fleet, he tried to win Athens to the Persian side, but failed. In the spring he again advanced into Attica ; the Athenians again removed their families, and sent to Sparta, urging the necessity of sending a force north of the Isthmus to help their chief ally. The Spartans can hardly have been without a strong desire to meet the Persians ; but circumstances made them act slowly and secretly, for Argos and Mantinea, guarding the two main roads north, were disaffected ; when they did move they had to make a wide detour to the west. Mardonius, on their approach, withdrew into Bœotia, where the ground was more suitable for his cavalry —the Greeks had none—and there encamped. He may have had about 150,000 men, with the addition of 30,000 to 50,000 medising Greeks, chiefly Bœotians and Thessalians. The force under the Spartan Pausanias numbered in all over 100,000, of whom 38,700 were hoplites, including 5000 pure Spartans —a large number. Again, there is much difficulty in ascertaining the exact details : it seems that at first Pausanias chose ground that was too open, and was harassed by the Persian cavalry, who at last cut off his water supply, and he retreated to a spot north-west of Platæa by night ; but in the night march the divisions lost touch, and in the battle next day the Greek centre took no part. On the left the Athenians, under Artistides, held the Greeks opposed to them ; but the real shock was on the Greek right, where the Spartans met the Persians. The latter relied on their masses : Pausanias withheld his charge till the ill-disciplined Persians, who had little defensive armour, were in confusion, and at the right moment led his men to the attack. The issue was never in doubt ; discipline carried the day, Mardonius was slain, and the Persians utterly broken. On the left the Athenians had the better of the Thebans, who, however, made good their retreat to Thebes. The other Greeks, on both sides, hardly took part in the fight, so that the Spartans and Tegeans on the one wing, and the Athenians on the other, deserve the whole credit of the victory.

The battle of Platæa was decisive ; Central Greece was at once won from the invaders, few of whom escaped, and the recovery of the North was only a question of time. Over 1800 years were to pass before an Oriental army again set foot on Greek soil. Thebes held out for a while, but the leaders of the medising party at last surrendered, and were executed.

On the same day as Platæa, says tradition, the

battle of Mycale took place across the Ægean. The Persian fleet had reassembled off Ionia, and the Samians and Chians sent to implore the Greek fleet, which lay at Ægina, to liberate them. Obviously it was not to the interest of the Athenians to destroy the Persian fleet before the Spartans had advanced north of the Isthmus; they might well suppose that if they had nothing to fear from the Persian fleet, the Spartans might revert to their Peloponnesian policy, and leave Attica in possession of Mardonius; and they may well have assured themselves that Pausanias was bent on a pitched battle before they sailed across the Ægean. On the approach of the Greek fleet, the Persians retired from Samos to Mycale, where they disembarked and entrenched themselves; but the Greeks followed them ashore, attacked them, drove them within their fortifications, and ultimately routed them in a bloody fight, in which the Athenians, under Xanthippus, gained the honours of the day. This victory gained for the Greeks the islands of the Ægean, and, with Platæa, assured them of respite from further attack for some years; of the great armament which Xerxes had collected two years before, there remained not enough even to form the nucleus of a future expedition.

Hardly less important is the great struggle in Sicily, where the Carthaginians, acting in concert with the Persians, were defeated at Himera by Gelo of Syracuse—on the same day as Salamis, according to tradition. Thus in both East and West the Greeks won for themselves liberty—the liberty freely to develop on natural lines.

IV.—THE ATHENIAN EMPIRE.

HERODOTUS ends with the Persian wars; and, for the history of the next fifty years, we are again left groping for facts, without which general theories are apt to be nebulous and unconvincing. This is the more to be regretted, because these years mark the rise of Athens to greatness. Sparta, Argos, and Corinth stand still: Thebes is discredited after her share in the Persian wars; but Athens stands out as the leader of Hellas against the Persian, becomes the mistress of the Ægean and the head of a maritime Empire, and develops a thoroughly democratic constitution; moreover, she not only leads Greece politically, but rises in the realm of literature and art to a height that has never been surpassed in the history of the world.

The liberation of their kinsmen in Asia from the Persian yoke was the chief concern of the Greeks after their own successful resistance to Xerxes. Pausanias, the victor at Platæa, at first commanded them; he conquered the greater part of Cyprus, an excellent point of vantage against the Phœnician fleet, and then turned to Byzantium in the northeast; but his arrogance and treasonable correspondence with Persia turned the allies against him, and he was recalled. When the Spartans sent out another commander, they found that the allies had handed over the command against Persia to the

Athenians, who thus reaped the reward of their great sacrifices on behalf of Greece.

Sparta, indeed, had enough to do in the Peloponnese. Pausanias was not the only instance of the incapacity of Spartans for distant commands. Leotychides, his fellow-king, had failed in an expedition to punish Thessaly for medism, and was condemned for taking bribes; he fled to Arcadia, and sought to revive the projects of Cleomenes, not without success. The spirit of independence had been fostered by the Persian wars, and democratic movements are found in the first half of the century at Argos, Elis, and Mantinea; and democratic means also anti-Spartan. After Platæa, Mantinea had resumed its Philo-Laconian policy for a time, but between 473 and 464 Sparta had to fight two great battles—at Tegea against the Tegeans and Argives, and at Dipæa against all the Arcadians except the Mantineans; the Spartans won both, and were again supreme in the Peloponnese, but in 464 a great earthquake ruined the town of Sparta, and a general revolt of the Helots followed, which took years to suppress. Argos, it will be seen, took no part in the battle of Dipæa, and thus lost a great chance; the destruction of the Dorian upper classes by Cleomenes in 495 had resulted in the admission of the lower to the franchise, and in the fifth century Argos becomes a democracy of the Athenian type. But the defeat of 495 had done more than that; it had destroyed the powers of Argos in its immediate neighbourhood, and Argos now pursued the shortsighted policy of reducing Mycenæ and Tiryns instead of striking at the heart of Sparta in conjunction with the Arcadians. This must have helped the Spartans, whose iron discipline enabled them to emerge successfully from all their struggles; it is no wonder, however, that they left the command against Persia to Athens, still a loyal member of the Spartan League.

Athens meanwhile had done nobly. No Peloponnesians helped in the subsequent struggles with Persia, but the rest of the maritime allies formed themselves into a league known as the Confederacy of Delos, under the protection of the Delian Apollo, whose temple was their treasury. Recognising the superior organisation and equipment of the Athenians, most of the allies preferred to pay a money contribution and to leave Athens to do the work ; the assessment of this was the work of Aristides, and the great general of the league was Cimon, son of Miltiades. This league was gradually resolved into an Athenian Empire ; attempts to withdraw from it were treated as rebellion, and dealt with accordingly ; eventually the treasury was transferred to Athens, and the allies were compelled to bring their suits to the Athenian courts. But this was not yet, and it is a mistake to suppose that Athens was from the beginning endeavouring to establish herself as an imperial state. Cimon, indeed, devoted himself whole - heartedly to the cause of Greece against Persia ; in ten years the coast-towns of Thrace and the whole coast line from Byzantium to Pamphylia were set free from the Persian yoke. Then Persia made a great effort, and equipped an armament, both naval and military, to act against the coast-towns ; Cimon met it off Pamphylia, drove ashore at the mouth of the Eurymedon and captured their fleet of 200 ships, then landed, and in a fierce battle utterly routed the Persian army. This battle (467) relieved the Greeks from apprehensions of attack for some years, and caused the Carian cities to join the league ; the revolt of Egypt in 462 further embarrassed the Persians.

The Athenians seem to have early become rather exacting ; and the possibilities that opened out before a genuine federation with some form of common citizenship were destined never to be realised : the basis of the league was narrowed, not broadened, and part of its strength was spent in the suppression of revolts from its authority. The reduction of the island of Scyros was justified, for it was a nest of pirates, and to police the Ægean was one of the first duties of the league ; but Carystus in Euboea was compelled to join the league—the first coercive step that Athens took. The important island of Naxos revolted, and was reduced (469), and after the Eurymedon Cimon had to spend over two years in reducing Thasos : it is significant that the latter applied for help to Sparta, which would, they said, have been given but for the Helot revolt. Soon Lesbos, Chios, and Samos were the only allies contributing ships and men on equal terms with Athens ; the result was to make the Athenian fleet a professional fleet superior to any that the Mediterranean had yet seen —Athens, that is, became at sea what Sparta was on land.

On his return from Thasos in 463 Cimon was accused on a political charge—the law courts played a great part in party politics—but was acquitted. To enable us to understand the coming changes in Athenian policy, foreign and domestic, some brief notice of the state of parties is necessary. After the changes wrought by Cleisthenes, the state naturally would take some time to settle ; there would not automatically spring up two parties with definite policies. The one stable element is the influence of the great families, two of which, the Peisistratids and the Alcmæonids, adopted revolutionary measures at the time of Marathon. That battle, fought under the auspices of the

young democracy, established the new constitution
once for all, and thereafter the power of the Peisistratids is broken, while the other two families, the
Philaidæ supported by Themistocles, and the Alcmæonidæ by Aristides, seem to be angling for the support
of the people ; but to label one of them conservative
and the other democratic seems to antedate a later
state of affairs. Between Marathon and Salamis
Themistocles prevailed and carried out his naval
policy ; but in the year 479 his rivals Aristides and
Xanthippus are at the head of affairs—a change for
which no authenticated explanation can be found :
it may have been due to the efficiency displayed by
the aristocrats at Salamis. Subsequent events, however, are not so doubtful. Cimon, son of Miltiades,
united the two families by his marriage with an
Alcmæonid, and this union was too strong for Themistocles, who, however, survived, and in some respects
did good service, till his ostracism in 471.

After the Persian wars, one writer says, the Areopagus
ruled Athens for seventeen years ; Cimon's party, that
is, finds strong support from the Areopagus, a council
recruited from members of the upper classes. This,
then, we may call the conservative or moderate party,
attached to the constitution, but opposed to innova-
tions. During Cimon's ascendancy there springs up
a second party, democratic or radical, led by Ephialtes, first organiser of the democracy that is now
beginning to realise its power : the trial of Cimon
(463) shows that a formidable party is arrayed against
him. This trial is further interesting as marking the
entry into public life of Pericles, son of Xanthippus ;
he has reversed his father's policy ; there is no room
for him on the aristocratic side while Cimon lives, so
he has joined Ephialtes and has thrown the influence
of the Alcmæonidæ into the democratic scale. Hence-

forth the two parties are fairly clearly defined, with
an oligarchic revolutionary party in the background,
which does not become prominent till Athens falls
upon evil days.

Themistocles had saved Greece, but his subsequent
history is rather melancholy. After the final defeat
of the Persians he did indeed succeed in rebuilding
the walls of Athens, in spite of Sparta's ill-judged
opposition, and in fortifying her harbour, the Peiræus ; but he did not bear prosperity well, and his
methods do not seem to have been above suspicion.
After his ostracism he was implicated in the treasonable correspondence of Pausanias with Persia, and
after some vicissitudes of fortune fled to Asia Minor,
where he lived at the expense of King Artaxerxes till
his death, always promising to win over Greece to
the Persian Empire, but never, so far as can be
seen, taking any steps to fulfil his promise.

Cimon prosecuted the Persian war unremittingly,
and assisted, perhaps unconsciously, in the trans-
formation of the Delian Confederacy into an Athenian
Empire. In Greece he recognised " spheres of influence "—to Athens the sea, to Sparta the land ;
and the value of this policy, soon to be overthrown,
was proved in later years. Though there are signs
that Sparta did not approve Athens' policy of coercion
in regard to the Confederacy, Athens was still a
member of the Peloponnesian League, and as such
was asked to send a force to help the Spartans against
the revolted Helots, who had fortified Mount Ithome
in Messenia. Cimon went in command of 4000
hoplites, but the Athenians, who had a reputation
for skill in siege-work, failed, and were abruptly dismissed. Nothing could have been worse for Cimon's
party : his failure put into power Ephialtes, with an
anti-Spartan and democratic policy ; Cimon was

ostracised, and the Areopagus, the stronghold of the
aristocrats, round which the struggle centred, was
deprived of its "guardianship of the laws," and reduced to the status of a court to try cases of homicide ;
this had been its duty from time immemorial. The
democratic substitute for this "guardianship" was
the Graphê Paranomôn, regarded as the Palladium
of Athenian liberties ; by this the proposer of a
measure which involved a change in any of the
established laws was liable to be prosecuted and
condemned to death ; the date of its institution is
unknown. Another democratic measure, introduced
about this time, was the law throwing open the
archonship to the third class ; it may be remarked
that technically the fourth class was never admitted
to the archonship, but in practice its members were
regarded as eligible.

Ephialtes did not enjoy his triumph long ; he was
assassinated—it is not known by whom—and the
leadership of the democrats passed to Pericles. The
war with Persia was carried on as before ; on the
revolt of Egypt from Persia the confederate fleet of
two hundred ships was sent first to Cyprus, then to
Egypt (459) ; but this expedition was unfortunate,
for five years later it was annihilated, together with
a relieving force of fifty ships, on the Nile. One
result of this disaster was the transference of the
treasury of the Confederacy from Delos to Athens ;
this step was taken on the proposal of Samos, in
fear of a Persian raid.

Before discussing the domestic policy of Pericles,
we must note the striking effects of the breach with
Sparta upon Athenian relations with the rest of
Greece. While Athens was a member of the Peloponnesian League, Corinth and Ægina had perforce
to endure the gradual transference of their Eastern

trade to Athens; now these old rivals combined in self-defence. At no time in Greek history is the inter-dependence of constitutional and political affairs more clearly shown. Athens opposed oligarchy, and strove to establish democracy wherever possible; her opponents relied upon oligarchy. Thus Athens allied with democratic Argos, and in Thessaly supported monarchy against oligarchy; and when Megara came to blows with Corinth over a frontier dispute, Athens received her with open arms, and so brought on the "First Peloponnesian War." The defection of Megara from the Peloponnesian League to the Athenian was of vast importance to Athens, owing to its strategic position on the lines of communication between North and South; moreover, Megara had a port on either side of the Isthmus, so that Athens now gained a foothold on the Corinthian Gulf. It was perhaps about this time (459) that the Spartans succeeded in taking Ithome; the defeated Messenians were settled by Athens at Naupactus, a harbour which commands the Corinthian Gulf near its entrance. Menaced on every side, Corinth allied with Ægina and Epidaurus against Athens, but the latter everywhere emerged successful. Ægina was reduced, and became a tributary of Athens; the Corinthians were defeated by Myronides, in command of the Athenian reserves. The successes of Athens against the members of the Peloponnesian League could not leave Sparta unmoved, and an army came north (457); after settling a quarrel between Phocis and Doris, the Spartans organised the Bœotian Confederacy, under the leadership of Thebes, on an oligarchic basis; this was no doubt intended as a counterpoise to the growing power of Athens on land. Then they turned south, and intended to act in concert with the oligarchic revolutionary party at Athens and to overthrow the democracy; but the Athenians barred their way at Tanagra, and a stubborn battle ensued. The Spartans secured their retreat, but it was a moral victory for Athens; an armistice was concluded, and thereafter Myronides marched into Bœotia, and won a great victory at Œnophyta; all Bœotia (except Thebes), Phocis, and Locris came under Athenian sway, and were reorganised on a democratic basis. Achaia also joined Athens.

The Athenians were now at the height of their power, and the democratic policy of a land-empire had so far been completely justified; but it was soon to be seen how slender were the foundations on which this empire was based: this policy demanded that either Athens must overthrow Sparta or *vice versâ*. Meanwhile they completed the Long Walls from Athens to the Peiræus—an attempt to overcome their natural disadvantages, and make Athens and the Peiræus practically one town, and that a seaport. A naval expedition burnt the Spartan arsenal and gained some successes in the Corinthian Gulf. Then came the first set back—news of the disaster to the Egyptian expedition. Pericles was unsuccessful as general in command of an expedition in the West, where Athens was still further trying to undermine the position of Corinth, and the tide of feeling began to set in favour of the aristocratic party. In 451 Cimon returned from exile,* and his policy gained the day; he made peace with Sparta for five years, and preparations were begun for an expedition against Persia, now dangerous after the reduction of Egypt. This was Cimon's last expedition: he died during the siege of Cition, either of disease or from a wound, but the Athenians defeated both the fleet and army

* The story of Cimon's earlier recall is based on unreliable evidence; his period of ostracism ended naturally in 451.

opposed to them before they returned home. There-after a convention was concluded with Persia—the Peace of Callias—whose details are obscure, but whose effect was to leave the Eastern Mediterranean to Persia and the coasts of the Ægean to Athens. Cimon died at the time of Athens' greatest power—a power which he himself had done much to raise; he had carried on the work of his father Miltiades and of Themistocles to a glorious issue, and after his death the story of Athens is one of diminishing power and influence; he had made of his city a world-power, but he left behind him no man with the will and the ability to continue his work, and Athens hereafter confines her efforts to the Greek world, and deals no more in international politics.

The Athenian land-empire fell at a blow; an Athenian army was cut off by the Bœotian oligarchic exiles at Coronea (447), and Bœotia was lost; with it naturally went control of Phocis and Locris. Eubœa and Megara revolted almost at once, and on the ex-piration of the truce in 446 the Spartans invaded Attica. Pericles was dealing with revolted Eubœa —an integral part of the Athenian Empire—but his diplomacy, or perhaps his bribes, persuaded the Spartan king to retire; peace was made, whereby Sparta sacrificed the interests of Eubœa, which was recovered; but Athens lost permanently Central Greece, Achaia, and (most important of all) Megara and its ports. Thereafter Pericles resigned all claims to the mainland outside Attica, and confined his attentions to the organisation and exploitation of the subject allies of the Delian Confederacy for the benefit of the Athenian citizen. Two measures of a popular nature are ascribed to him—one, limiting the citizenship and its privileges to those whose parents were both Athenian citizens (451 B.C.); the

other, the introduction of the system of pay, for
service in the law courts, the Boulê, and in war.
The first was distinctly demagogic, as its first exer-
cise shows. In 445 the king of Egypt, revolting from
Persia, sent a gift of corn to Athens with a plea for
help ; a revision of the register was made, and 5000
citizens struck off the roll !—Limit the number of
citizens, and increase each man's share. So, too,
with the system of pay, perhaps necessary when instituted ; but it lends itself to abuses, and we cannot
wonder that Pericles' opponents spoke of it as bribing
the people with their own money. With these measures we must compare the treatment of the allies.
There was no longer war with Persia, and the Confederacy had fulfilled its purpose : what was to hap-
pen to it ? A permanent fleet was necessary, for
war might break out again, and perhaps the suppression of revolts from the league might be justified ;
but was it justifiable to maintain the tribute on a
war footing, and spend the balance on the beauti-
fication of Athens ? It was on these points that
Pericles' policy was challenged, but a vote resulted
in the ostracism of Cimon's successor as leader of
the aristocratic party, Thucydides, son of Melesias,
probably in 442 ; and for the next ten years Pericles'
position was unchallenged. Athens was adorned with
temples and statues, literature and art rose to their
height ; and meanwhile the Empire was seething with
discontent, for, in Pericles' words, the Athenians held
it as a tyranny. Athenian citizens were sent out to
Eubœa, Thrace, and the Black Sea, and acted not
only as colonists but as garrisons. The chief revolt
was that of Samos (440), which took nine months to
suppress.

V.—THE PELOPONNESIAN WAR.

THE Peloponnesian War marks a new era, not in Greek history, but in our knowledge of it. The historian's business is no longer to attempt to determine the accuracy or inaccuracy of disputed facts, but to determine what principles underlie the facts presented to him. This change is due to the genius of Thucydides, the first historical critic, and a study of his history, with the work of Grote as commentary, is indispensable to a thorough appreciation of the state of Greece, and of Athens in particular, at this time. Detailed criticism is naturally impossible here; a brief summary of the most important events of the war, and a few of the most obvious comments, are all for which room can be found.

The events that led up to the war may be briefly stated. Since her defeat in 457, and the loss of her eastern commerce, Corinth had devoted her energies to the West, and was occupied in building up an empire round the Ambracian Gulf; hence when in 440 Sparta proposed to help Samos, revolted from Athens, Corinth objected, saying that it was for each state to deal with its revolted allies. But in Corcyra, which commanded the route westward to Tarentum and Syracuse, the democratic party secured the upper hand, and quarrelled with Corinth; a bitter struggle ensued, and Corcyra sought the aid of Athens. Anxious to increase her influence in the

West, Athens made alliance : hence Corinth failed to defeat Corcyra at sea (432), and her commercial existence was seriously menaced. War between the rival leagues was now inevitable ; Sparta was urged on by Corinth, who would otherwise have seceded, for the struggle was one of life or death to her ; sentiment also demanded that Corinth should assist her colony, Potidæa, revolted from Athens. The famous Megarian decree, by which Athens excluded Megara from commercial intercourse with all ports in her empire, may be regarded as an ultimatum from the side of Athens, and in 431 war began. Thucydides regards it as having long been inevitable, and says that the deep and growing hatred of Sparta for Athens made it merely a matter of time as to when war should break out ; but this opinion must be questioned, for, granting the Spartan dislike of all forms of tyranny, the fact remains that the Athenian Empire had begun to decline, and that Spartan and Athenian interests did not clash in any quarter, as they had done while Athens held a land-empire ; indeed, there was a strong party at Sparta opposed to the war, and ready to make peace at the first opportunity. The early operations tend to show that at first Corinth, not Sparta, was the real protagonist on the Peloponnesian side.

Sparta was a military, Athens a naval power ; it is therefore clear that Sparta could only attack Athens in so far as Athens was vulnerable by land, and Athens could only harm Sparta in so far as Sparta was vulnerable by sea. Attica itself, and the subject-cities of Thrace, were thus open to attack by Sparta. Attica was regularly raided (for Athens no longer held Megara), but no attempt was made on Athens itself—the Spartans were quite unequal to the task of storming the strong Athenian walls, and never attempted it; the vulnerability of Thrace was a later discovery, but while attacks upon it had considerable effect on Athens, they were by no means decisive. On the other hand, any substantial success that Athens could gain over Sparta must be gained by land—a highly improbable contingency; her fleet could cause considerable inconvenience to Sparta, and could sweep from the seas the fleets and commerce of the maritime members of the Peloponnesian League. But without some change in these conditions it is evident that no decisive blow can be dealt; one of the belligerents must challenge the supremacy of the other in the peculiar province of the other— Athens must become strong by land or Sparta by sea, otherwise the war becomes a mere contest of endurance; hence the indecisiveness of the first part of the war (431–421). In the second half Sparta is found in possession of a fleet, paid for by Persian money; Athens is defeated in her own element, and the war is brought to a definite conclusion (413–404).

Pericles' plan of campaign was purely defensive; he determined to treat Athens within the walls as an island, abandoning Attica to the enemy, and sending away the flocks and herds to Eubœa; supremacy at sea was to be maintained, a firm hold to be kept of the allies, and occasional descents to be made on the Peloponnese by way of reprisals. But Athens was not an island; great material loss was caused by the sacrifice of the farming class to the commercial, besides the moral effect, which must have been very considerable on so excitable a people; we cannot wonder at the cowardice they afterwards displayed at Delium. Moreover, the Peloponnesians had no resources to exhaust as Athens had, so this cautious policy was distinctly one-sided.

This plan was, however, carried out for the first

few years. Attica was raided by the Peloponnesians ; Thebes was allowed her revenge by the blockade of Platæa, which was razed to the ground ; a destructive plague, vividly described by Thucydides, invaded the crowded streets of Athens. True, the revolts of Potidæa and of Lesbos had been suppressed, but at the price of the exhaustion of the treasury ; the only success had been two great naval victories achieved by the Athenian admiral Phormio at Naupactus. Pericles' popularity had not survived the plague ; he was brought to trial and fined, but recovered his position, only to die in the same year (429). Athens had suffered most, Corinth a little, Sparta not at all. Athens, it seemed, could do no more at sea than she was doing, nor Sparta by land ; the war was becoming a contest of endurance, rather to the detriment of Athens, but the years 427–423 show a change on her part to a more vigorous policy.

Of the two parties at Athens, the conservative or moderate, headed by Nicias, desired peace at any price ; the radical, led by the political Cleon and the general Demosthenes, was ready to try any promising scheme, and this party gained the day. Distant expeditions were undertaken, and Athens began to use her army to support her fleet. Sparta she could scarcely attack, but the Corinthian Empire in the north-west was soon shattered ; Demosthenes, aided by his Acarnanian allies, crushed the Ambracians in two battles, in spite of Spartan support, and Corinth was completely ousted from that district. Two expeditions sent to Sicily to destroy Corinthian commerce and establish Athenian influence gained no notable success. Their third scheme, the establishment of an effective blockade of the Peloponnese, was fairly successful, and led incidentally to one of the most decisive actions of the war. Demosthenes was fortifying Pylos in Messenia, and the Spartans endeavoured to take his fort ; a number of them crossed to the island of Sphacteria close by, where they were cut off by the Athenian ships. The Spartans immediately sent proposals for peace to Athens, but Cleon rejected them, and eventually nearly 300 pure Spartans were captured—useful hostages for Athens, and a great blow to Spartan prestige. This refusal of terms by Cleon is noteworthy, for had peace been made then, it would have appeared that the Athenian Empire was invulnerable, while by her successes in the north-west and at Pylos the balance of the war had inclined in favour of Athens. But Cleon, the first of the demagogues, could not see any further ahead than the immediate present ; Athens was exhausting her resources with little profit to herself, and in 425 the tribute of the allies had to be doubled. The demagogues were indeed almost wholly responsible for the continuation and ultimate result of the war ; led away by hope, inspired by any success, they insisted on pursuing an aggressive policy, and formulated grand schemes which exhausted the revenues of Athens. They were honest men, but, drawn from the mercantile class, were entirely uneducated in politics and deficient in political imagination. Peace in 425 would have given Athens time to recover, both in money and men ; moreover, it would have rendered the position of Sparta precarious, by accelerating the democratic movement in the Peloponnese and Bœotia, and the capture of Megara would have left Attica safe.

For the democrats in Megara were now (424) willing to hand over the city to Athens, and had partly succeeded when the Spartan Brasidas intervened, and put the oligarchs again in power, so that Megara was lost to Athens. This was the turning-point of the war. A more ambitious scheme of the radicals was the restoration of the Athenian land-empire in Central Greece by the aid of the democratic parties; a rather complicated scheme of invasion was formed, but it miscarried, and at Delium (424) the Athenian troops showed cowardice, and sustained a severe defeat. Most damaging of all, however, was the expedition of Brasidas to the Thracian province. This the Athenians might have secured once for all by the help of their powerful ally, the king of Thrace, who, in the early years of the war, overran Macedonia with a great army, and, if supported by Athens, might have crushed the deceitful Macedonian king and restored the power of Athens over the towns of Chalcidice; but they neglected this chance, and now paid the penalty. Brasidas was the one great Spartan produced in this first half of the war; he saw that Amphipolis, guarding the only bridge over the Strymon, was the key to the situation; his eventual aim was perhaps the Hellespont and By-zantium, the capture of which would have starved Athens, whose corn came from the Black Sea. Taking advantage of the prevailing discontent, he annexed town after town on his rapid march, even-tually securing Amphipolis without a blow; the Athenians failed to use their sea-power to trans-port troops to garrison the endangered towns, and for this neglect Thucydides the historian, who com-manded the Athenian squadron off Thrace, was punished with exile.

The year 424 had been disastrous for Athens, and an armistice for a year was concluded with Sparta. Cleon, however, persuaded the Athenians to send him to regain Amphipolis, and in 422 he met Brasidas in battle outside the walls. Both were slain, but Brasidas was victorious. The two generals, the chief obstacles to peace, were, however, removed, and in 421 the Peace of Nicias was arranged. Athens agreed to give up the posts that blockaded the Peloponnese in return for the Chalcidic and Thracian cities.

The peace lasted eight years, and when war broke out again it took on quite a different complexion; nevertheless Thucydides counts it as part of the same war, so that it is traditionally known as the second half of the Peloponnesian War. To understand its character we must consider the events which led up to it. On the conclusion of peace, Sparta and Athens formed a treaty of alliance, presumably on the Cimonian basis of "spheres of influence." This endangered the existence of the Peloponnesian League. Corinth had lost by the war; she was hostile to the terms of peace, for her existence was at stake, and war against Athens was for her almost a necessity. Bœotia, Megara, and the Chalcidians in the north supported her. Deserted by Sparta, this group applied to Argos, whose thirty years' truce with Sparta was about to lapse. But there was amongst Sparta's allies another discontented group; the position of some of the philo-Laconian oligarchies in the Peloponnese was becoming critical, and Elis and Mantinea were now democratic; their natural ally was Argos, which again aspired to supremacy in the Peloponnese. Had these two groups combined against Sparta her position would have been impossible. But the pronounced oligarchies of Megara and Thebes would not co-operate with so pronounced a democracy as Argos, and by repudiating the Athenian alliance the Spartans could easily detach the oligarchic group, which was not hostile to Sparta herself, but to her philo-Athenian policy. An excuse for this measure was ready to hand; Sparta could not against their will deliver

up the Chalcidian and Thracian cities to Athens, so
Athens refused to evacuate Pylos and Cythera, and
in 420 the Ephors practically repudiated the alliance,
and the Corinthian group returned to their allegiance.
Sparta was now free to deal with the Peloponnesian
democrats, but the decisive action did not come till
418, when, at the battle of Mantinea, the Argives
and Mantineans were defeated—Elis was foolishly
fighting elsewhere for her own hand—and Sparta
regained the prestige which had been lost at Sphacteria, and her position as unquestioned head of the
Peloponnese.

Meanwhile at Athens parties had been evenly
balanced. The conservatives were seen to have
made the peace at the wrong time, and after the
failure of Sparta to fulfil its terms, Nicias' position
was shaken, and the radicals carried the day and
formed an alliance with Argos. Their leader, Alcibiades, had in 419 a triumphal diplomatic progress
in the Peloponnese. He was a nephew of Pericles,
an Alcmæonid, brilliant, ambitious, and unscrupulous
—the most prominent citizen of Athens in the fifteen
years that preceded her fall. His policy—actively
to support the Peloponnesian democrats against
Sparta—was good if taken up strongly ; but the
balance of parties was very even ; neither could remain in power long enough to give Athens a consistent policy, and in the critical year (418) the
conservatives were again in power, so that Athens
lost a splendid opportunity of crushing Sparta at
Mantinea.

Thereafter, the conservatives endeavoured to carry
out their programme—the maintenance of the Empire intact—and sent expeditions to Thrace to recover
Amphipolis, but without result. The Athenian
citizen-soldier, tired of hard campaigning in a Thra-

cian winter, was now ready to listen to the more
attractive programme of the radicals, which was a
natural outcome of their Sicilian project of 427.
Athens had long looked westward with eager eyes,
and a Sicilian expedition offered many advantages ;
to secure a commanding position there would damage
Corinthian trade.   Sicily was one of the three corn-
growing districts of the ancient world, one of which,
Egypt, was now closed to Athens, while communications with the other, South Russia, were difficult to
maintain ; but what most attracted the Athenians
was the prospect of increasing their Empire, and main-
taining themselves on the proceeds.   Their immediate
prospects of success were good ; the fall of Syracuse,
which should have been effected, would probably
have meant the submission of all Greek Sicily and
Italy ; but behind these looms the grim figure of
Carthage, hostile to everything Greek, and even
then girding herself for an aggressive war against
the Sicilian Greeks.   Athens was overtaxing her
strength ; her financial position was unsound, and
to meet it her subject allies were being exploited ;
particularly in men was she unequal to the task she
had set herself ; and further, the aggrandisement of
Athens in the west could only result in deeper enmity
at home.   Such indeed was its immediate effect ;
Alcibiades, the real leader of the expedition (which
apart from its results to Athens belongs rather to
Sicilian history), was recalled almost at once on a
charge of sacrilege.   He escaped on the way home,
made his way to Sparta, and persuaded the Spartans
to adopt the two most damaging measures yet taken
against Athens—the sending of a Spartan commander
to Syracuse and the establishment of a permanent
garrison at Decelea, in Attica, overlooking Athens.
The Corinthians were also urgent that Sparta should

again declare war to aid Syracuse and to maintain Corinthian interests in the west, and the Athenian programme, as stated by Alcibiades—to win the west and use the resources thus acquired for the acquisition of a hegemony over the whole of Greece —made the Spartans, whose interests and prestige were now threatened, take up the war in deadly earnest.

The determining factors of this second war (413–404) are easily seen. Athens was sorely weakened by the total loss of her best fighting men ; both the first expedition under Nicias, and a relief expedition of almost equal strength under Demosthenes, were totally destroyed at Syracuse ; the oligarchic party once more began to raise its head, the allies began to revolt, and the state of Athens seemed desperate. But in spite of internal troubles, disaffected allies, and an exhausted treasury, Athens could well have held out had this war continued on the same lines as the former ; the city was proof against Spartan armies, and fleets could be built to hold in the allies. The new feature is Spartan naval enterprise, hitherto impossible because Sparta had no trade, and so no financial resources ; but now, with the practically unlimited resources of Persia to draw upon, Sparta could fit out fleet after fleet, and thus meet Athens on her own element at an advantage. This immoral alliance between Sparta and Persia was suggested by Alcibiades, who thus dealt his country a still greater blow ; into the tortuous negotiations which followed it would be unprofitable to enter ; the alliance was eventually carried out whole-heartedly by Lysander, the great Spartan admiral, and Cyrus, younger son of the Persian King Darius. Persia, it seems, was to recognise Spartan hegemony in Greece, provided that the Ionic cities should again become Persian tributaries, as before the Persian wars.

Politics at Athens and Sparta, the intrigues of both with Persia, the chequered career of Alcibiades as political adventurer, all have an influence upon the operations of the war, which, however, is simple in its main outline, and depends on two alternating considerations—the capacity of Athens to rule the Ægean and Propontis sufficiently to reduce her revolted allies and protect the convoy of grain-ships to Athens ; and the capacity of Sparta to defeat the Athenians decisively enough to secure the command of the sea, and so to starve out Athens.   Hence the important battles are naval, and take place mostly in the Hellespontine region, with Byzantium, the key of the Black Sea, as the prize of the victor.

The Athenian headquarters was Samos, now democratic and a strong supporter of the Athenian democracy ; in this war the old struggle between democracy and oligarchy is very pronounced. Samos was a useful post for watching Persian intrigues, and centrally situated as regards the Empire, whose subjects were revolting in large numbers. While the fleet was at Samos, the oligarchs at Athens carried through a revolution, established themselves in power as the Four Hundred, and opened negotiations with Sparta ; they were perhaps ready to give up the city. The fleet at Samos disowned them, and a naval defeat off Attica, followed by the revolt and loss of Euboea, discredited them ; democracy was restored, and the army in Samos recalled Alcibiades, now regarded as the sole hope of salvation for Athens. Henceforth operations are clearer ; Mindarus, the Spartan admiral, makes for the Hellespont, threatening the very existence of Athens ; he is partially defeated at Cynossema (411), and next year utterly crushed at Cyzicus in the Propontis. This victory, due largely to the skill of Alcibiades, gave the Athenians a splendid chance of recovery, for Sparta offered peace ; but the demagogue Cleophon persuaded them to reject it. For a time Athens was comparatively successful, and several revolted allies were reduced ; then Cyrus came down from Persia to Ionia, Lysander was appointed Spartan admiral, and the tide turned. At Notium, near Ephesus, the Athenians were defeated (407) ; Alcibiades, whose lieutenant was responsible, was disgraced ; he retired, and was eventually murdered ; his brilliant gifts, which might have done so much for Athens, had been used rather to ruin his country. In 406 Callicratidas succeeded Lysander, but after defeating the Athenian Conon, he was himself defeated at the Arginusæ Islands, near Lesbos, by a fleet that represented the last great effort of Athens. Peace was again offered by Sparta, and again refused—a crowning folly—by the influence of Cleophon. Demoralisation had set in ; the generals who had fought at Arginusæ were put to death because they had neglected the duty of recovering the corpses of the slain ; and the fact that a fleet of 180 ships could still be sent out from the exhausted city shows her immense vitality. But in 405 Lysander was again in command ; again the Hellespont was the point of attack ; and the crushing defeat of Ægospotami left Athens to the mercy of the victor, who starved the city into submission, and entered it in 404.

The terms granted were generous ; the Corinthians and Thebans demanded the destruction of Athens ; but Sparta was content to have the Long Walls razed, and to set the city under the oligarchy that had long been intriguing for such a consummation, and gained an unenviable notoriety as the Thirty

Tyrants. Critias, their leader, was the Robespierre of the Reign of Terror that followed ; in the end he was slain in battle by the democratic exiles under Thrasybulus, and the Spartan King Pausanias restored to Athens her democracy.

VI.—SPARTA AND THEBES.

IN one sense the Peloponnesian War marks the climax of Greek history, and the fall of Athens is its great tragedy. Athens has, most of all the Greek states, captured the imagination of succeeding ages; it is to Athens, and especially to Athens of the fifth century, that men turn for the literature and art that has made Greece famous; and from this aspect Greek history seems to lose its light when the rise, the brief glory, and the fall of Athens have been recorded. But this point of view—sentimental perhaps, but pardonable—obscures the true place of Greece in universal history: to safeguard the Western civilisation they had formed, and to propagate it throughout the known world, was the true mission of the Greeks; and in their relations with the East the great importance of their history lies. From this aspect the Peloponnesian War is only one of that series of internecine feuds that prevented the complete unity of Greece at the time of Xerxes' invasion, and continued to hamper and degrade the relations of Greece with Persia until unity was imposed from without by the power of Macedon, and Greece proper became almost the least important part of the Greek world. But of these struggles it is the most important and the most typical, and as such has been given what might seem a disproportionate amount of space, that the lesser struggles which follow may be more briefly dismissed. Like them, its ultimate result was to weaken the Greek power of resistance to outside aggression, and the first half of the fourth century is the most humiliating time of Greek history, from the point of view of Greek relations with Persia.

Sparta, the professed champion of autonomy, now borrowed from Athens her imperialistic ideas; the Athenian Empire became a Spartan Empire, with oligarchy as its basis. But the Spartans, avaricious and bullying by nature, could not rule free men, and this state of affairs did not last long. Moreover, Spartan ambitions were too great for their strength; they were soon, as champions of Greece, involved in war with Persia; there were complications in the Peloponnese; and a league of Corinth, Argos, Thebes, and Athens, to preserve the balance of power, resulted in the Corinthian War, of which Sparta had by no means the better. Eventually the Spartans came to terms with Persia, and the humiliating Peace of Antalcidas (386 B.C.) was arranged, Persia acting as the arbiter of Greece; its basis was that of complete political independence for each city, with Sparta as the hegemon or leader of Greece: the Greek cities in Asia were ceded to Persia.

The causes of Sparta's failure—a failure soon to be more pronounced—are easily seen; they had a limited population and insufficient resources (even after the exploitation of their new empire) for a transmarine war, which was largely a matter of money. And in Greece itself war was changing; it was becoming an art, and mercenaries were taking the place of the citizen-army. Soon there were to be other professional armies besides the Spartan; and while Sparta lost citizens on whom the life of the state depended, hired mercenaries cost nothing

but money to those who could afford them. Iphi-
crates discovered the value of light-armed troops,
properly manœuvred, and did great harm to the
Spartan heavy-armed.

There is a further reason for Sparta's ill-success
against Persia : her armies were usually victorious
in Asia Minor, but they could never take the field
in sufficient numbers while disaffection lay behind
them in Greece : and one of the notable features of
this period is the insistence upon the balance of power.
So soon as one state gained some pre-eminence, a
combination was formed to prevent its further aggrandisement, and so the larger states of Greece are
worn out by gradual attrition, until they fall a comparatively easy prey to Macedon. In this process
Persia played a part : Persian diplomacy helped to
form the league against Sparta : Persian ships,
under the Athenian Conon, destroyed the Spartan
fleet at Cnidus (394), and so cut off the army of
Agesilaus in Asia : and when Sparta was sufficiently
reduced, Persia admitted her once more to alliance,
for a military power with little naval strength did
not seem so dangerous as one equipped with a fleet
that might harass her coasts.

Persia was indeed much concerned to keep her
Greek neighbours employed amongst themselves :
an incident at the beginning of the century had
shown the inherent weakness of her military position.
Cyrus, the friend of Lysander, had rebelled against
his brother Artaxerxes, and marched almost up to
Babylon before his rashness cost him his life at
Cunaxa. In his army were 10,000 Greek mercenaries,
who carried all before them, and after the battle made
their way, in spite of opposition, northward through
difficult territory till they reached the Black Sea
at Trapezus. This is the famous Retreat of the

Ten Thousand, described by Xenophon, their leader, and it appealed strongly to the imagination of the Greeks; it had much to do with the abortive attempt of the Spartan king Agesilaus to conquer Asia Minor, and is the natural prelude to Alexander's conquest of Persia.

After the Peace of Antalcidas Sparta confined her attentions to Greece proper; her supremacy was thoroughly established in the Peloponnese, and Mantinea and Phlius harshly treated. The citadel of Thebes was seized and held for three years: and in the north the promising Chalcidian federation was broken up. Thus for a time Sparta used her power tyrannically, but forces were rising which were to overwhelm her. Conon's great victory at Cnidus had begun the revival of Athenian power: her walls had been rebuilt, and some of her former subjects returned to their allegiance. A new confederation was formed to which Thebes, recovered from Sparta by Pelopidas, lent her name: its purpose was to secure political independence, and it was defensive in character; so it was in no sense an attempt to re-establish the Athenian Empire. In the war which followed Sparta undertook operations by land and sea; but her invasions of Bœotia were uniformly unsuccessful, and an attempt to cut off the Athenian cornships and starve the city led to the disastrous battle of Naxos (376), in which Athenian naval supremacy was once more asserted. This led to a great extension of the Athenian confederacy; but funds were lacking for a protracted war, and eventually Athens made peace with Sparta in 371, on the old basis of " spheres of influence "; Sparta practically renounced all claims to suzerainty by sea, and Athens largely recovered the position lost in the Peloponnesian War. It was a tribute to the hard work and ability of her statesmen, backed by the resources of a commerce that the great war had done little to destroy.

But Athens and Sparta could not now divide the Greek world as they had done for a century : two other powers stood in the way. Thebes had been excluded from the recent treaty because Epaminondas, her leader, claimed to take the oath on behalf of the Bœotian Confederacy, which Sparta refused to recognise ; and in the north Jason of Pheræ, a despot whose ambitions aimed at the enforced unity of Greece under his own rule and the conquest of Persia, extended his sway over all Thessaly, and with his well-organised army became a Hellenic power. Jason allied with Thebes, which was immediately attacked by Sparta ; but at Leuctra Epaminondas defeated the superior forces that were ranged against him, and Spartan military supremacy was overthrown. He massed his forces in a solid body, fifty deep, and routed the twelve-deep formation of the Spartans, who had no cavalry to assist them : 1000 fell, including 400 pure Spartans.

Jason of Pheræ secured the retreat of the Spartans, whom he did not wish to see entirely crushed, and took the opportunity to seize Thermopylæ, the key to Central Greece ; but next year he was assassinated, and his power, which was based entirely on his personal ascendancy, died with him.

Thebes was therefore left supreme, and a new alliance between Sparta and Athens could not alter this. It was now the aim of Epaminondas to secure the power of Thebes by checking Sparta in the south, and by preventing the rise of any new power in the north. The battle of Leuctra led to the overthrow of philo-Laconian oligarchies in the Peloponnese ; Mantinea rebuilt her walls, and Arcadia formed a federal league with its centre at Megalopolis, a city founded to be the federal capital and to guard the western passes from Laconia. The adhesion of Tegea to this league led to an abortive expedition under Agesilaus ; this was countered by a Theban invasion under Epaminondas (370). Laconia itself was attacked for the first time in history, but Sparta could not be taken. Messenia, however, was rendered independent, and the city of Messene founded to act as its capital—but there was no federation : Messene was the only city in the new state. The great possibilities that had lain before Sparta for two centuries were now at an end ; had she adopted a liberal policy of enfranchisement much might have been accomplished : but that was contrary to the Spartan character, and now constant warfare, and the growth of large estates owing to increasing wealth, had diminished the number of her full citizens to about 1500 ; for only those who had a certain amount of land could claim citizenship. The loss of Messenia greatly accelerated this process, and yet the Spartans, who lacked elasticity, made no attempts at constitutional reform.

Athens, anxious for the balance of power, aided Sparta, and an attempt was made to find a basis for peace : but Sparta demanded Messenia, and Athens Amphipolis, dreaming of a new empire, so Thebes objected : the question was referred to Persia, who decided in favour of Thebes, but the allies refused the terms.

Sparta was now disabled, and the Peloponnese a confusion of quarrelling states : Arcadia caused much trouble with its shifting policy, and eventually the Arcadian League split, owing to the old rivalry of Tegea and Mantinea. Mantinea allied with Sparta, who was joined by Elis, and eventually in 362

Epaminondas made his last expedition to reduce the Peloponnese once more to dependence upon Thebes. At Mantinea he defeated the combined forces of the Spartan alliance in a great battle, but met his death, and his most trusted subordinates also fell. In the peace that followed, the independence of Megalopolis and Messenia was recognised, but in this Sparta refused to join.

Before estimating Epaminondas' statesmanship we must consider his work in the north. In Thessaly Thebes strove to establish a balance by supporting a Thessalian federation against Alexander of Pheræ, Jason's successor, who was helped by Athens; in this he was assisted by the rising power of Macedon, hostile to Athenian pretensions to Amphipolis; indeed, Athens, who had regained Samos and was occupied in the reduction of Chalcidice, was now Thebes' chief rival in Greece. Fearing Athenian designs on Eubœa also, Epaminondas resolved to create a fleet, which was instrumental in detaching some members of the Athenian alliance; but the Theban fleet never became a real force. The Thessalian problem was eventually solved by the reduction of Alexander of Pheræ, who was defeated at Cynoscephalæ by Pelopidas, the former deliverer of Thebes from Sparta, and with Epaminondas the creator of Theban power; but in the battle he met his death (364).

With the death of its two creators, the real power of Thebes came to an end. It had been based on a foundation less secure than even that of Sparta, which relied on a small military caste; and when the personal ascendancy of Epaminondas was removed, Theban supremacy faded almost as quickly as that of Jason of Pheræ. Epaminondas was a great soldier, but no great statesman: the age-long aim of Thebes, the unification of Bœotia, was still unrealised, and with no national Bœotian sentiment to support him, he had to rely on a military autocracy. His attempt to create a fleet in a country which had no commerce was doomed from the first to failure. His work in the Peloponnese must judge him, for that alone had any permanence : Arcadia and Messenia remained independent. His aim, as in all things, had been to secure the headship of Thebes, and to that end he had destroyed the old supremacy of Sparta ; but to substitute for it a quarrelling collection of small states was a step backwards. Epaminondas' work was in fact purely destructive in its results, and he showed no capacity for constructive statesmanship.

VII.—MACEDON.

THE failure of Sparta and Thebes was due to the lack of resources both in men and money. So long as the citizen-army was everywhere the rule and campaigns were short and decisive, Spartan discipline and concentration prevailed; but soon distant and more extended campaigns were required, demanding resources that Sparta did not herself possess and found it difficult, with her lack of commerce, to acquire; this, and the growth of a class of professional soldiers, determined her ultimate downfall. The brief supremacy of Thebes was due almost entirely to a single man; when his commanding influence was removed, his city sank again to its normal position. Neither city had, nor could create, the resources to hire troops and build fleets; they had no commerce. Athens is in a somewhat different position; it is because of her resources that she is enabled still to hold up her head; and her naval power rested on a more secure commercial basis than the ephemeral fleets of Sparta and Thebes. But in the lack of far-seeing statesmanship Athens also shared; a democracy, whose policy varies according to the party in power, must needs be lacking in the consistency that is so valuable an element in a nation's foreign relations. Themistocles, probably the greatest of Greek statesmen, had realised both his city's capabilities and her limitations: Cimon had followed in his path : Pericles had realised Athens' limitations perhaps more than her capacities, and had narrowed her sphere of influence : but succeeding politicians had been unable to remain in power long enough to carry through a definite and consistent policy. So Athens frequently overstrained her resources, and a period of excessive energy had to be followed by one of recuperation.

The new power that was destined to supersede all these rivals was based on more solid foundations. In brief, it was a military despotism, sufficiently provided with men and money, and so containing in itself the resources and the centralisation that were necessary to carry out a firm and consistent policy. First as regent, then as king, Philip of Macedon laboured for twenty years, until, by force and diplomacy, by intrigue and violence, he at last became the master of Greece. As a hostage in Thebes, he had in his early years acquired a knowledge of Theban strategy and an insight into the workings of Greek diplomacy ; he realised the possibilities, and determined to raise his half-Hellenic nation to a position no Greek state had yet achieved. In its full details it is a fascinating if complicated story ; but the main outlines are clear.

Philip accomplished two great works : the organisation and development of his own kingdom, and the extension of his power in an ever-widening circle through Greece till Thebes was conquered and Athens humbled. To the actual kingdom of Macedon, extending some sixty miles to north and west of the Thermaic Gulf, was added from of old the suzerainty over the hill-tribes of Pæonia in the north and Lyncestis and Orestis in the west. This suzerainty Philip determined to convert into direct rule ; he remodelled and trained his army, and met with great success, taming the Pæonians and winning a great victory over the Illyrians of the west, who were a frequent source of trouble. Thereafter he proceeded to create a " professional army with a national spirit " from the excellent material which he now had to work upon, and the result is the evolution of the famous Macedonian phalanx. Armed with a longer spear, and arrayed in more open order than Epaminondas' hoplites, the phalanx depended less on mere weight, and was more capable of movement; and to win his battles Philip depended equally on his large body of heavy cavalry, which was the " crack regiment " of the Macedonian army. To pay troops was a difficult matter for a country that had no commerce; Philip made up for this deficiency by seizing the gold mines of Mount Pangæus, across the Strymon, so that now Macedon was equipped with the three desiderata of Greek warfare—trained troops, resources, and a single will to direct them.

It was in the matter of Mount Pangæus that Philip first came into contact with the older powers of Greece. After the death of Epaminondas Thebes had faded; Athens had recovered Eubœa and Sestos, and established herself once more as mistress of the Ægean. She had power round the Thermaic Gulf and in Chalcidice, and desired Amphipolis, the key of Thrace. But Amphipolis was necessary to Philip, for it guarded the route to Pangæus, and his seizure of it (357 B.C.) was the beginning of the end of Athenian power in the north. In the south also Athens fared badly; inspired by the Carian Mausolus, Chios, Cos, and Rhodes revolted; Athens lost the two generals, Chabrias and Timotheus, who had chiefly built up her Second Empire, and the loss of these islands was permanent; soon the Chersonese and Eubœa alone were left to Athens, for Philip had

destroyed all her power in the Thermaic Gulf by
353. His foundation of Philippi secured Mount
Pangæus on the north.

Philip now turned south, and entered Thessaly by
request, to defend it from the Phocians. They had
established a short-lived but remarkable supremacy
in Central Greece, depending on the possession of the
treasures of Delphi, which were used to hire mercenaries. Driven to this originally by the aggression
of Thebes, Thessaly, and Locris, who had used against
them the Amphictionic Council—a Pan-Hellenic body
for the government of Delphi—their leaders, Philo-
melus and Onomarchus, extended their power from
the Corinthian Gulf to the north of Thessaly. Onomarchus even defeated Philip, whose forces were
inferior in numbers, in two battles, but next year
(352) Philip returned. Onomarchus was defeated
and slain, and Phocis was only saved by the prompt
action of Athens, who sent a force to guard Thermopylæ. Philip was for the time content to con-
solidate his power in the north; the Chalcidian
League was the next to succumb; Olynthus, its
chief city, was taken in 348 in spite of Athenian help.
Finally, in alliance with Thebes, Philip secured the
much-coveted pass of Thermopylæ, the key to Central
Greece, which he entered with an army, nominally to
punish the Phocians for their sacrilegious use of the
Delphic treasures.

Philip was more than a military adventurer; he
was a Hellene in spirit, and desired to be recognised
as such by the older states of Greece, whom he
wished to lead against their age-long enemies of
Persia. For this the co-operation of Athens, whom
he always treated with great respect, was desirable,
but the determined hostility of the orator Demosthenes blocked the way. The brilliance of his

speeches has blinded historians to the fact that Athens was not naturally Philip's enemy, but modern criticism is beginning to reconsider his position and to give him lower rank as a statesman.

Macedon was a land power, and its natural enemy was rather the land power of Thebes, which stood in the way of further advance, than the sea power of Athens, which might well be its ally in greater things. So thought Eubulus, whom Demosthenes opposed, and peace was made in 346. But Athens was divided, and pursued no firm policy, sulking when Philip, who had been given a place on the Amphictionic Council—thus securing his recognition as a Hellene—presided at the Pythian games.

After the assertion of Macedonian supremacy in Epirus, Philip proceeded to establish his power in Thrace, which became a tributary of Macedon; this affected the Athenian command of the route of the Black Sea, and attacks on Perinthus and Byzantium led Athens, inspired by Demosthenes, to declare war. His eloquence and energy patched up an alliance with Thebes, who had indeed the greater reason to fear his presence in Central Greece. Philip marched southward at once; and at the famous battle of Chæronea (338) the hegemony of Greece passed definitely to Macedon; the Theban Sacred Band died fighting, and Thebes was crushed. Athens, the other combatant, was admitted to an advantageous peace, while the citadel of Thebes was garrisoned. Philip displayed his power in the Peloponnese, and called a congress at Corinth, where, next year, he was appointed general to lead the Greek forces against Persia. His garrisons at Corinth, Ambracia, and Chalcis showed that he had no illusions as to the capacity of the Greeks for united action, and were a proof that Greek political independence in the older sense was a thing of the past. But Philip was not destined to attack Persia; he was assassinated as the result of a quarrel with his wife. He had accomplished a great work, without which Alexander's exploits would have been impossible, and the greatness of his statesmanship is beyond question.

With Alexander we leave the heated atmosphere and confined scope of Greek politics for a wider stage; and in this case more than in any other, apology is needed for thus "in little room confining mighty men." The briefest chronicle of his deeds is all that can be given, and the barest estimate of his aims and character.

Alexander had first to assert himself in his own realm; he defeated the northern tribes, and penetrated to the Danube, then punished the Illyrians in the west, turned to disaffected Greece, and destroyed Thebes, the centre of disaffection; thereafter he was free to attack Persia. In 334 he crossed the Hellespont to Asia Minor, and sacrificed on the site of Troy. His army of some 40,000 was met by a slightly larger Persian force containing many Greek mercenaries, whose leader, Memnon of Rhodes, advised the Persian generals to retreat before Alexander, draw him from his base, and cut his communications—a plan all the easier because the Persians commanded the sea. They insisted on meeting him, and were decisively beaten on the banks of the Granicus. The Greek cities of Æolis and Ionia were liberated, and democracies established; serious resistance was offered only at Halicarnassus, where Memnon had taken refuge. He had a scheme for organising the Ægean against Alexander, which might have proved serious in view of the latter's weakness in naval forces; but his death at the critical moment relieved the position. Alexander, however, had grasped the fact that command of the sea could be won on land, and determined to master the whole coast line of the Eastern Mediterranean. His army concentrated in Phrygia, passed the Cilician Gates, and advanced towards Syria, where Darius, king of Persia, awaited him with a large force; Alexander routed him at Issus (333 B.C.), and proceeded to occupy Syria and Phœnicia; in subsequent negotiations he refused Darius' offer to cede all land west of the Euphrates. The Phœnician city of Tyre took seven months to capture, and then his road to Egypt lay clear; here he was welcomed as a deliverer, and made an expedition to the oracle of Zeus Ammon in the desert, where the priest hailed him as son of the god; and he founded the city of Alexandria, destined to take the place of Tyre as the chief commercial centre of the Eastern Mediterranean.

With nothing now to fear by sea, Alexander could strike at the heart of the Persian Empire. He advanced without opposition till he reached the Tigris, and at Gaugamela, some sixty miles from Arbela (from which the battle is usually named), scattered the vast Persian host (331). Darius fled to Media, but Alexander marched south and east to secure Babylonia and Persia, seizing vast treasures at Susa and Persepolis. Next year he went in pursuit of Darius, occupied Ecbatana—whence his rival had fled—and secured Media: the breathless chase went on till at the Caspian Gates Darius was overtaken— dead, for his cousin Bessus had slain him as the conqueror appeared in sight.

The north-east hardly proved so easy a conquest; Bessus set himself up as king, and organised a national resistance in the home of the Iranian race—Parthia, Aria, Bactria. Alexander had to fight no pitched battles, but when he had conquered the first two provinces and advanced into Bactria, a revolt in Aria caused him to return. This crushed, he made a wide eastward detour, eventually entering Bactria early in 328 over the Parapamisus (Hindu Kush) from the south-east, after wintering in the Kabul valley. Bessus retreated over the Oxus into Sogdiana, where he was taken and put to death. This year was spent in reducing the provinces north of the Hindu Kush, and in 327 the advance to India began.

Alexander spent the summer fighting the hill-tribes to the north-east, and in the spring of 326 crossed the Indus by a bridge which he had had built in the previous year. Of the three kings of the Punjab, one joined him and one remained neutral; the third, Porus, he defeated on the Hydaspes in the severest battle he had yet had to fight. Porus became his ally, and Alexander advanced to the Hyphasis; there, however, with the rich country of the Ganges almost in sight, his army refused to advance any further, and the long eastward march was ended. The three kings were left to govern the conquered lands east of the Indus, while the west was left in Macedonian hands. Alexander himself set out to explore the Indus to its mouth, conquering the tribes through whose territory he passed; part of his forces he sent westwards by the more northerly route; he himself traversed the inhospitable wastes of Gedrosia, and rested in Carmania before advancing once more to Persepolis. The fleet, which had accompanied him down the Indus, sailed under the command of Nearchus along the coast till it came to the entrance to the Persian Gulf, and thence to the mouth of the Euphrates.

Questions of government and the organisation of his vast conquests employed Alexander for a year. Meanwhile at Babylon a fleet of 1000 ships was being prepared for purposes of exploration ; Alexander himself was to lead it, but four days before the time appointed a drinking-bout led to the fever which carried him off at the age of 32.

It is not strange that historians have differed widely in their estimate of Alexander's policy and its influence. He has ceased, it is true, to be regarded merely as the " Great Emathian Conqueror " ; but while some see little but good in the change he wrought in the world, others lament his attempted extension of Greek civilisation to the East ; it was but a debased Hellenism, they say, that he propagated, calculated to benefit neither the Eastern Greeks nor the races with whom they mingled. Some note of his character and aims will show why this opinion is rather to be rejected.

Alexander was by birth and education a Hellene ; it was not for nothing that the great philosopher Aristotle was his tutor. In his character he combines the best virtues of the best Greeks—an exceptional combination, in fact, of the man of action and the idealist, uniting in himself, as no man of his opportunities has ever before or since united, imagination and capacity for action and government. He was a tremendous worker ; his conquests were so rapid that one is amazed to read that organisation went hand in hand with them. His insight into the character, not only of men, but of peoples, was sure, and determined the measures that he took in different provinces to suit their particular needs. His nature was straightforward and trusting, and singularly free from vice. One tyrannical act—the execution of his general Parmenio, whose son was found conspiring against him—is recorded against him, and one or two indiscretions, such as the murder of his friend Cleitus in a fit of drunken madness. This leads us to the reverse of the picture ; his natural pride was increased by his rapid conquests, and he demanded to be worshipped as a god not only by Orientals, but by his Macedonian nobles, who rightly resented the claim, and objected to his adoption of Oriental dress and customs ; neither can entirely be defended on grounds of policy, for he had not the opinion that the Persians were naturally a nobler nation than his own, and therefore to be imitated.

But in its aims, and in most of the measures he took to carry it out, his policy was sound and practicable. His leading idea—the amalgamation of Greek and Persian—runs through almost every measure. In the army a place was given to Persian troops. He founded as many as seventy cities, which, beside their natural advantages as fortresses and trade-centres, aimed at promoting a settled life in the country. He wished to persuade the Persians to abandon their half-nomadic habits and adopt the Greek city life to some extent. In the organisation of the provinces he adopted no cast-iron imperial system, but varied his form of government to suit local customs and requirements. He encouraged his men to take Persian wives, and himself married Persian princesses. By these measures he strove to banish that rivalry between East and West which was already beginning to disappear. In Western Asia Minor mixed marriages had taken place before his time, and the results had not been noticeably bad ; he endeavoured to overcome all opposition to them, with such success that Greek civilisation was predominant in Asia Minor for centuries after his death.

To the purists who maintain that he destroyed the fine flower of Greek civilisation, which could flourish nowhere but on its native soil, it may be answered that the bloom had already fallen, never to be recaptured, if indeed it ever existed elsewhere than at Athens in her prime, and Athens was now toiling, and continued to toil, in the arid wastes of philosophy and rhetoric. The more solid advantages of Greek civilisation, trade and commerce, law, and the Greek "way of life" were as ready of growth in East as in West, and to Alexander it is due that Greek influence pervaded the East, while Greece itself "is praised and starves." Had he lived to complete his work of organisation, Greek civilisation might have endured as long in his Eastern as in his Western conquests: dying at an age when most men have but begun their public life, he still could claim to have extended almost to an infinite degree the horizon of Europe.

VIII.—THE GREEKS IN THE WEST.

OF the settlements of the Greeks in the West some account has already been given in Chapter II. ; they divide naturally into three groups—those in the bay of Naples, of which Cyme was the chief : those of Southern Italy, and those of Sicily. Of the first two groups no connected history can be given, at any rate in earlier times. Little opposition seems to have been offered to their establishment by the native tribes, whose pursuits were of the primitive agricultural type. Cyme, the outpost of Greek civilisation, was apparently on good terms with the Etruscans, the early masters of Campania, whose activity precluded further advance ; and the states of Southern Italy soon became prosperous both by agriculture and by commerce (p. 23). Such contests as are recorded are between Greek and Greek ; early in the sixth century Croton and Sybaris combine to destroy Siris, and Locri and Croton are at war. The most notable antagonism, however, is that between Sybaris and Croton, when the latter, led by the athlete Milo, defeated the Sybarites and razed their city to the ground (511 B.C.). In this century Magna Græcia was, like Ionia, the home of philosophy ; Pythagoras flourished at Croton and Metapontum, Xenophanes established the Eleatic school.

The history of Sicily is at once fuller and more

important. There are two epochs when Sicily has played a great part in the history of the world—when it has been the meeting-place of East and West, when the ancient Greek has maintained his hold against the Phœnician, and the mediæval Christian against the Mohammedan ; at other times Sicily sinks into insignificance. The questions that interest in Sicilian history are therefore connected with " foreign " politics, and constitutional questions are largely absent ; with the necessity for centralised power to meet the barbarian, tyrants and mercenary troops take the place of the oligarchy or democracy and the citizen armies of Greece proper—a change easier to understand in newer communities which had no immemorial constitutional traditions.

The two great non-Greek powers of the West, Carthage and Etruria, are found combined against the attempted Phocæan settlement in Corsica (circ. 540), but except for one other notable instance, which will be recorded in due course, the Etruscans were not, apparently, aggressive. But when the power of Carthage had grown by commerce and agriculture in Africa, and she had assumed the protectorate of the Phœnician settlements that already existed in the West of Sicily, contact with the Sicilian Greeks became inevitable, and intermittent wars on a considerable scale continued until both Sicily and Carthage fell before the power of Rome.

Possibly the earliest Sicilian tyrant, Phalaris of Acragas (circ. 560), was a champion of Greek against Carthaginian ; but the great war of 480 B.C. is the first recorded struggle. Phœnician and Greek had always been antagonists in trade, and there can be little doubt that the Phœnicians, who formed the backbone of Xerxes' fleet, instigated their Carthaginian kinsmen to attack Sicily in the year of the great Persian expedition. As against Xerxes, the Greeks were not united; most of the Sicilian cities were under tyrants, the greatest of whom, Gelo, had succeeded to the tyranny of Gela, and had recently secured without a struggle the greatest of Sicilian cities, Syracuse, which he made his capital; with him was allied his father-in-law, Thero of Acragas. Against these were ranged the two tyrants of Himera and Rhegium, the latter of whom was also in possession of Zancle, whose name he changed to Messana. Terillus of Himera, driven out by Thero, appealed to Carthage, and King Hamilcar landed with a great host and advanced to recover Himera. Gelo's seasoned mercenaries met him there, and utterly defeated him in a great battle; Carthage was granted terms, and the peace endured for seventy years—a contrast to the activity of Athens and her allies after 479 which will be understood if it be remembered that the Sicilian tyrants had to consider their private interests, which would not be served by driving Carthage to extremities : and they had no Asiatic kinsmen to deliver from the barbarian yoke.

Gelo's brother and successor, Hiero, is famous for his court, which was the resort of poets such as Æschylus, Pindar, and Simonides, and for his great victory over the Etruscans at Cyme in 474 B.C. For some fifty years Cyme had been engaged in intermittent struggles both with the Etruscans and with the native inland tribes ; her preserver, Aristodemus, obtained the tyranny, and there was peace for a time with Etruria ; but after his murder the aristocratic government was hard pressed by the Etruscans, and appealed to Hiero for aid. He was a man capable of taking a broad view of the obligations of Greek to Greek ; the great victory which he won perhaps marks the beginning of the decline of Etruscan power; certainly they molested the Greeks no more. Cyme survived till well into the next century, when it fell to the native Samnites, and lost importance.

The successors of Hiero and Thero were incapable, and democracy succeeded tyranny almost throughout Sicily. The shiftings of population from one city to another which had been indulged in by the tyrants—acting perhaps on the model of the Assyrian and Babylonian kings—and the disbanding of their mercenaries, made the settlement of Sicily difficult at first; but the cities soon began to enjoy great prosperity. This was momentarily endangered by the genius of Ducetius, a Sicel chief who succeeded in uniting for a time the scattered native communities of the interior. Acragas was only saved from him by Syracuse, but eventually he was defeated. He was allowed to retire to Corinth, whence he returned and founded a colony on the north coast. His aim was to establish cities on the Greek model, and he was partially successful, but with his death, in 440, all hope of an independent Sicel nation vanished. The Sicels still held the interior, however, and later were useful allies to the Athenians.

The Ionian cities in the West had long been overshadowed by the Dorian; and Athens, supreme in the Ægean, but ever ready to extend her own influence, was anxious to gain ground in the West, where Peloponnesian, and especially Corinthian, sympathies naturally predominated. Pericles' colony of Thurii, near the site of Sybaris, failed in its object, for it soon became Dorian in character; then a treaty was made with Rhegium and Leontini in 432, which, on the outbreak of a quarrel between Leontini and Syracuse, led to two ineffective Athenian expeditions in 427 and 425. These were, in fact, the means of reuniting Sicily, and the Congress of Gela, moved by Hermocrates of Syracuse, proclaimed the doctrine of " Sicily for the Sicilians."

The reasons for the great Sicilian expedition have already been given (Chap. V.) : its occasion was a quarrel between the non-Greek city of Egesta, whose cause Athens espoused, and the Dorian Selinus ; the real objective was Syracuse, leader of the Dorians. Many years of comparative peace had left the Syracusans unprepared for a great war, and the magnificent Athenian armament might have taken the city almost without a blow, had they listened to Lamachus, the practical soldier who was joined with Nicias and Alcibiades in the command. Nicias had opposed the whole project, and Alcibiades was now anxious to display his diplomatic talent ; he carried the day, but before he could do anything was recalled to Athens. This much diminished the prospects of success, and when the rest of the summer was frittered away, the Syracusans, who at first had been panicstricken, began to despise the Athenians ; they did not, however, neglect the opportunity of improving their fortifications.

The story of the siege is told at length in Thucydides VI. and VII. ; the bare outline only can be given. In the spring of 414 the Athenians attacked Syracuse, captured the plateau which commands the city, and proceeded to invest it. A single wall was carried round it, and two counter-walls built by the Syracusans were taken and destroyed ; but the second attack resulted in the death of the energetic Lamachus, and Nicias, instead of pushing on operations, proceeded to double half his wall, while the other half was still unfinished. He kept a poor watch, and Gylippus, the Spartan sent by Alcibiades' advice to command the Syracusans, was allowed first to

land in Sicily, and then to enter Syracuse, just when
the citizens were about to surrender. This was the
turning-point : the energetic Spartan persuaded the
Syracusans to meet their enemies in the field, where
they were victorious, and carried a third cross wall
past the Athenian lines, thus rendering Syracuse
practically safe against the present investing force ;
he stirred up the neutral or disaffected states of the
south to send help, and inspired the Syracusans to
man a fleet and try their fortunes at sea. Nothing
went well for the Athenians, and Nicias was compelled to write to Athens begging either leave to
depart, or large reinforcements. An expedition
almost as imposing as the first was equipped and
sent under Demosthenes and Eurymedon—the former
the ablest Athenian general of his day. He examined
the ground and determined to try a night attack on
the cross wall, and, in the event of failure, to retire
forthwith. Nearly successful, the attack was wrecked
by one of the misunderstandings common in night
attacks ; but Nicias would not retreat at once—he
hoped still that the philo-Athenian party would surrender the city to him. At last he was persuaded,
but an eclipse of the moon intervened, and his " seer "
prescribed a wait of " thrice nine days." Then it
was too late : the Syracusans, who before would
gladly have seen the Athenians go, had now determined to block the harbour-mouth, attack them by
land and sea, and destroy the whole armament. So
it came to pass : in two great battles in the harbour
the Syracusan fleet was victor ; when the Athenians
strove to retreat by land to the interior they found
the passes blocked ; they were divided, cut off from
supplies and water, and those who were not slain
surrendered. Nicias and Demosthenes were put to
death, the rest sent to the quarries to live in foul

conditions which soon killed them off; some few escaped.

In the pride of their victory the Syracusans made their constitution still more democratic, and gave help to Sparta against Athens; but soon all their strength was needed to combat a new invader. Carthage, quiescent for 70 years, now aimed at complete supremacy in Sicily; her policy is definitely imperialistic; and henceforth, for over 150 years, Sicily is the scene of intermittent conflicts between Phœnician and Greek, leading to the titanic struggle between Rome and Carthage which was to determine the supremacy of the Western world—a struggle in which Sicily was to be first the battle-ground, then the prize of the victor. The occasion of her invasion was the old quarrel of Selinus and Egesta. In 409 Hannibal, grandson of the Hamilcar who perished in 480 at Himera, landed in Sicily with a large host: in nine days Selinus was stormed and sacked; death and slavery were the lot of its inhabitants. Himera was next attacked and stormed; Hamilcar was avenged, and the Carthaginians now held the west of Sicily from Selinus to Himera. Three years later Acragas was assailed, and after a siege of eight months taken; large Greek forces came to its aid, and the Carthaginians were sorely tried; but they held on, and fortune favoured them. The Acragantines eventually deserted their city in a cowardly manner.

Evidently some central power was needed to stay the power of Carthage, and this was found in Dionysius of Syracuse, who, by the usual devices—accusations of treachery, intrigue, the formation of a body-guard—rose to the tyranny. He failed to relieve Gela, which fell to Carthage, with Camarina. A pestilence in the Carthaginian camp saved Syracuse from attack, and by a treaty (405) Dionysius ceded to Carthage possession of the Western province and tributary rights over Gela and Camarina ; he himself was acknowledged master of Syracuse, and the other cities of Sicily were declared free.

Dionysius is a remarkable character : crafty, unscrupulous, and capable, he held the tyranny for nearly forty years, in spite of wars, revolts, and sedition. Moreover, he made Syracuse the greatest European city of his time ; he formed alliance with Sparta, extended his power into Italy, and stood forth—his chief claim to gratitude—as champion of Greek against barbarian. His four wars with Carthage were not uniformly successful ; the first (398–7) nearly destroyed him, but ended in a striking victory and a great reduction in Carthaginian territory, which passed to Dionysius, including all the cities taken by Hannibal and Himilco. His new subjects gave him trouble : Acragas proclaimed its independence, and the Sicels were insubordinate ; his settlement of barbarian mercenaries in Greek territory, and his arrogant pretensions, roused up enemies everywhere, and Carthage again took the field (392). Aided by a Sicel " tyrant," Dionysius held his own, and the war ended without any important change.

In the next few years Dionysius reached the summit of his power : he took Rhegium and the " toe " of Italy, thus commanding the straits, and gained great influence in the Adriatic and the west of Greece. His attempt to expel the Carthaginians entirely from Sicily (383 foll.) was, however, unsuccessful ; he was severely defeated, but not crushed, and escaped by surrendering the west of Sicily nearly up to Acragas, and paying an indemnity of 1000 talents. At the time of his death he was engaged in his fourth war with Carthage, which led to no change of territory.

His son, Dionysius II., reigned for ten years, at first supported by his uncle Dion, who induced him to try to rule according to the ideals of the philosopher Plato, whom he summoned to Syracuse. Then both Dion and Plato were banished; but Dionysius was not fitted for the tyranny, and in 357 Dion returned, collected troops, and expelled him. The record of the next thirteen years is one of strife and confusion, during which tyrants rise and fall, and the distinction between Greek and barbarian is almost obliterated. Finally, in 344 the Syracusans turned to Corinth, their metropolis, and asked her to send them a man to restore to the city her liberty. Timoleon, who came in answer to the call, was already old, but showed such vigour, capacity, and public spirit that his name is one of the most famous in Sicilian history. His task was immense, but he succeeded in all that he undertook. Landing with a small force, he took part of Syracuse; his opponents were leagued with Carthage, who sent troops and invested him. Timoleon's party grew in strength, the Carthaginians withdrew, and the rest of the city fell to the liberator. Dionysius, who had regained the tyranny, thereupon retired to Corinth and lived as a private citizen.

Freedom was thus restored to Syracuse; the city was so wasted by incessant war that an appeal was made to Greece for new citizens, and 60,000 are said to have answered the call. Timoleon thereafter restored to the other cities of Sicily their freedom and their Greek life, so far as was possible after the elder Dionysius' changes and settlements of barbarian mercenaries, many of whom were now driven out. Finally, when the Carthaginians once more attempted to regain their power in Sicily, Timoleon met and defeated them in a great battle at the Crimisus (339); peace was made, and the

Carthaginian province reduced to its former limits ; Gela and Acragas were restored. Timoleon retired into private life, and died at Syracuse in 336, the object of universal mourning.

After his death faction again broke out in Syracuse, only to be resolved by another tyranny—that of Agathocles, a capable soldier risen from the lower classes (317). In four years he secured the leadership of Sicily for Syracuse, but again came into conflict with Carthage ; he was defeated, and Syracuse besieged. In these straits he determined to create a diversion : he boldly crossed into Africa, where for three years he met with great success, but was eventually defeated, and returned to Syracuse, leaving his army to surrender in Africa. He had, however, shown the vulnerability of Carthage, and in later times the Romans profited by this lesson. The Carthaginians made peace, and were again confined to their province in the West. Agathocles continued in the tyranny till his death, in 289 ; the last fifteen years of his rule were, it is said, mild, and gave much-needed prosperity to the island ; and he successfully championed the Greeks of Italy against the Italians of the interior.

The confusion that followed Agathocles' death was ultimately resolved by the First Punic War and the absorption of Sicily by Rome. Tyrants sprang up, the Mamertines—Agathocles' Campanian mercenaries—established themselves at Messana, and Carthage began again to take the offensive. In these straits the Greeks appealed to Pyrrhus, King of Epirus, the knight-errant of his time. He had crossed to Italy at the request of the Tarentines, who had fallen foul of the Romans, now in contact with the Greek cities of Magna Græcia ; in two battles, at Heraclea and Asculum (280 and 279 B.C.), he had defeated the Romans; but his victories were "Pyrrhic victories"—he had lost more than he gained by them. Crossing over to Sicily, he was eminently successful against the Carthaginians, and took the title of King of Sicily; this estranged the Greeks, and after two years he returned to Italy, saying that he left Sicily as a wrestling ground for the Romans and the Carthaginians—a true prophecy. His third battle against the Romans, at Beneventum (275), ended in defeat, and he withdrew to Greece, where he continued to be a disturbing influence in politics till he was slain in the Peloponnese in 272 B.C. A remarkable character, brave, able, and ambitious, he lacked the constancy of purpose which might have made him a second Alexander.

The departure of Pyrrhus left the south of Italy to Rome, into whose hands Tarentum fell in 272, and Rhegium next year. Fresh discords arose at Syracuse, to be quelled by Hiero, who became first general, then king of Syracuse, and won victories against the Mamertines. In 264 the Romans entered Sicily as allies of the latter against Carthage, and the great struggle began which was to determine the rule of the Mediterranean. Hiero at first allied with Carthage, but next year changed, and to his death was a firm and useful ally to Rome. After the First Punic War all Sicily, save Syracuse, came under the sway of Rome, and became the first Roman province. Hiero lived till 216, the vassal-king of Rome; thereafter Syracuse became embroiled with the Romans; with the siege and capture of the city in 212 departed the last vestiges of Greek liberty in Sicily.

IX.—MACEDON, THE LEAGUES, AND ROME.

In view of the general Hellenic tendencies of Alexander the Great, and of his reverence for Athens in particular, one might perhaps have expected a great and immediate expansion of Hellenism over his newly won Empire. True, the following age is called the Hellenistic age, and most of the East was permeated by a form of Greek culture inferior to that of Hellas, but vivifying and inspiring ; in the domain of government, however, in which the Greek felt most at home, the Empire remained thoroughly Macedonian. Monarchic it had been in its inception, and monarchic it remained ; there was no place for the Greeks in the government of the East, and those who settled in the new conquests turned their energies into the more profitable channel of trade and commerce. During the struggles between his captains—the Diadochi—which followed Alexander's death, the home Greeks were for the most part pawns in the game. Athens enjoyed great prestige, but little power ; one party would proclaim the freedom of the Greeks, another would garrison their cities. In the height of this confusion the veteran politician Demosthenes, ever the rigid foe of Macedon—and in his later years with better reason—died for his political faith.

Into the struggles of Alexander's generals it is unnecessary to enter ; they were conducted purely for personal aggrandisement, and have no distinguishing features. At first there was a pretence that the Empire was being kept up for Alexander's posthumous son by Roxana, but this was soon dropped, and nearly all the Macedonian royal family —men, women, and children—met a violent end. Eventually dynasties were founded either by the generals or their sons. In Macedon itself Antigonus Gonatas, a grandson of one of Alexander's generals, established a dynasty which lasted till the absorption of Macedon by Rome. In Egypt Ptolemy, another general, reigned almost from the first, and from his descendant, Cleopatra, Egypt was at last taken over by Augustus ; never Hellenised, Egypt became more and more oriental, except for the Greek colony at Alexandria, whose great library is one of the features of the age. The Alexandrine school produced perhaps no first-class poet save Theocritus—a Sicilian— but in the domain of scholarship and science accomplished much. In Syria and the East Seleucus, accounted the most capable of Alexander's generals, founded an Empire which reached originally to the Indus, and had its capital at Babylon ; gradually, however, the native races resumed control of the Eastern provinces, till in time the Parthian Empire extended to the Euphrates—the boundary in later times of the Roman Empire ; but even then Greek civilisation, which had a fascination for the oriental, largely predominated in Parthia. The north and west of Asia Minor were split into several kingdoms : those of Attalus at Pergamum and Mithridates in Pontus were the most important, though Armenia, Cappadocia, and Bithynia all play a part in later history.

The Greek states were helped in their struggle for independence by an invasion of the Gauls similar to that which took place in the Italian peninsula in 390 B.C., when Etruria was overrun and Rome burned. In 279 they overran Thrace and Macedon, and next year descended into Greece; accounts are obscure, and the truth is difficult to come by, but it seems that the Greeks combined to make a successful resistance at Thermopylæ, and, after failing in an attempt on Delphi, the Gauls withdrew. Probably their incapacity to attack cities—they had no artillery and little protective armour—rendered them powerless against the walled towns of Greece; and though Thessaly with its plains proved an easy prey, there was little plunder to be obtained in the mountains of Central Greece. Antigonus Gonatas got the better of them in Macedon, and established his dynasty there; but a body of Gauls obtained a footing in the central plateau of Asia Minor, and eventually, after years of marauding, settled in the country called from them Galatia.

From this point the states of Greece resume their former course. Macedon is again a semi-alien power, always a decisive political factor in great struggles, but never again the master of the destinies of Greece. The Greek more than most men is " a political animal," and the chief interest that remains in Greek history is that of their last political experiment— the Achæan and Ætolian Leagues. Monarchy, aristocracy, oligarchy, timocracy, tyranny, democracy —Greece had tried all, and decided in the main— contrary to her philosophers—for democracy ; now an attempt was once more to be made at Federation. In a sense the Peloponnesian League had been a federation—a combination of states bound to act together politically ; but the central power of Sparta had been too strong, and not always equitably exercised—there had been too little equality. The

Delian Confederacy had been organised for a particular purpose—resistance to Persia. In the achievement of that purpose it had been transformed into the Athenian Empire. Now in the constitution of the Achæan League the component states had equal rights and duties, voluntarily contracted ; they acted in concert, while preserving each its own internal constitution. With the strong Greek instinct for local autonomy, this system should have been particularly suitable ; but the federation was too loose and ill-defined. The right of secession, of making separate treaties, &c., was unsettled, and the leagues were too much at the mercy of a chance majority. Moreover, the leading states held aloof, thinking of the hegemony which had been theirs in times past, and unwilling to make one of such a combination. The leagues, however, were successful in asserting the freedom of their constituents at a time when individual cities were too weak to assume that hegemony, and so served their purpose. In practice the personal element preponderated, as almost always in ancient Greece : an Aratus or a Philopœmen could always get his measures passed and secure his own appointment to carry them out.

The rise of the Achæan League to importance is in fact the work of Aratus of Sicyon, who liberated several cities from tyrannies (including Corinth and Megara) and added them to the league ; politically he was allied with the naval power of Egypt, while Macedon made friends with the Ætolians, who were in possession of almost all Central Greece. This comparative balance of power, which lasted for some time, was disturbed by a revolution in Sparta. Cleomenes III. fell foul of the Achæan League, and, after several victories, converted his state into a democratic monarchy ; the Ephors were killed, the second king deposed, the Gerousia abolished, the Periœci admitted to citizenship, and the old Spartan training reintroduced. With his attractive socialistic programme, Cleomenes detached several members from the plutocratic Achæan League, of which he now claimed the headship. Aratus was compelled to apply to Macedon for aid; the price paid was Corinth and the leadership of the league. Cleomenes was defeated at Sellasia (222), and fled to Egypt; his work in Sparta was undone. The Achæan League practically lost its independence, and the Macedonian king proclaimed an alliance of the Greeks with Macedon at its head. This the Ætolians refused to join: in the ensuing war they held their own, and in 217 made an honourable peace. Aratus, who had lived to see the destruction of his work, was poisoned by Philip of Macedon in 213.

The period from 220–146 marks the intervention of Rome in the affairs of Greece. Before the Second Punic War the Romans had established themselves on the east of the Adriatic, and the Greeks had not been able to hold aloof from the struggle between Rome and Carthage. Their alliances had, however, neutralised one another. Macedon and the Achæan League supported Carthage; the Ætolians and the Southern Peloponnese supported Rome. These two parties fought one another without any decisive battles, and the most noteworthy result of the conflict is the reorganisation by Philopœmen of the Achæan League and its forces; henceforth it appears once more as an independent and active power.

In the first instance Rome's intervention was decidedly beneficial: it served the general interests of peace, and in particular assured the freedom of the individual Greek states, at least for a time. The natural attraction for the Greeks of Rome and the Roman constitution was thrown into relief by their antipathy for the Macedonian monarchy, especially as represented by the selfish and unreliable Philip. It was from his aggressions that war began; the pacific powers of Pergamum, Rhodes, and Athens —all important in commerce—were allied with Rome; Philip's Eastern and Ægean ambitions brought him into contact with them, and an attack by him upon Athens led to a declaration of war by Rome. In the ensuing struggle Macedon at first held its own; but in the decisive battle at Cynoscephalæ (197 B.C.) the Roman maniple asserted its supremacy over the phalanx, and Philip was crushed.

The result to Greece was momentous. Macedon ceased to be a great power, and the Roman victor, Flamininus, proclaimed at the Isthmian Games the independence of all Greek States that had been dependent on Macedon; some joined the Achæan League, some the Ætolian. It now seemed as if Greece, under the ægis of Rome, was about to begin a new era of freedom and progress; yet within fifty years both leagues were conquered and suppressed, and the whole peninsula came under the direct government of Rome.

The reason was that the Romans, while professing —and no doubt feeling—unbounded admiration for the Greeks and their civilisation, were unwilling to let slip the real for the ideal; their strong practical common-sense told them that they had not liberated Greece from Macedon for the Ætolians to intrigue against Rome with the sovereigns of the East, or for the Peloponnese to be the theatre of continual petty warfare between the Achæans and Sparta. Rome is by no means free from blame as regards the details of her policy, but she could not be expected to forego her own interests and pursue a sentimental policy of non-intervention ; and at the first touch of the strong hand reaction sprang up in Greece.

The Ætolians, indeed, had done good service at Cynoscephalæ, and considered that in the final settlement the Achæans, who had joined the Roman alliance later, had received a preferential treatment beyond their due. Hence they welcomed and supported Antiochus of Syria, who proposed to make himself lord of all the Greek-speaking states. He landed in Greece, but found the Achæans and Macedon firm in their allegiance to Rome ; a Roman army defeated him at Thermopylæ, and a further defeat confined him to his Syrian possessions. The Ætolian League ceased to exist (189).

Philip of Macedon was succeeded by Perseus, who endeavoured once more to make head against Rome. His final defeat at Pydna in 168 ended the kingdom of Macedon. The anti-Roman party in the Achæan League also suffered, and a thousand hostages were taken to Rome, where they remained seventeen years. On their return they aroused their countrymen, already smarting under the dictatorial measures of Rome, and in 146 war was declared. It could have but one end : the battle of Leucopetra, and the sack of Corinth by Memmius and his troops, mark the end of Greek freedom.

Rome made no effort to supplant Greek civilisation and culture, but rather encouraged it, giving it organisation and new life, and ensuring its continuity ; only from the domain of practical politics were Greeks excluded, and Greek activity henceforth turned largely to commerce and the development of Asia Minor. The effect of Greece upon Rome was perhaps stronger and more lasting : Roman literature owes everything to Greek, and in art, science, and philosophy of every kind Rome is merely the disciple ;

Athens becomes, in fact, the university of the Roman world. That the effects of the reaction of the East upon the Roman character were bad admits of little doubt; but that is not the fault of the Greeks: rather must it be set down to the Eastern monarchies, with their aggrandisement of the individual. Rome had grown too rapidly, conquests had been too easy, and conquered lands too rich; it was in his Eastern campaigns that Lucullus pointed the way for Pompey, Cæsar, and their successors to emulate the monarchs of the East.

But if Rome gained much, if her conquests were rendered easier and the problem of governing them was simplified by finding a homogeneous civilisation in the East, yet this very advantage had also its drawbacks. Greek civilisation was not decadent but active, and there were elements in it which Rome could not assimilate. Already by the time of Antony and Cleopatra there are signs of the incompatibility of East and West in the Roman Empire. The division of that Empire by Diocletian accentuated what was already obvious: the thought and language of the East was always Greek, and the Byzantine Empire becomes Greek in its outward form as well as in its essence. As such it kept the flag of the old civilisation flying against the Eastern barbarian, as Greece had done against Persia centuries before, until the fall of Constantinople in 1453 A.D. ended at once the ancient and the mediæval world to begin the modern.

BIBLIOGRAPHY.

THE student cannot do better than begin with the article in the *Encyclopædia Britannica* on "Greek History" by the Rev. E. M. Walker (to whose lectures and essay-notes the present writer is much indebted) : many other articles—*e.g.* that on "Ægean Civilisation"—will be found of great value. Of Greek authors Herodotus should be read : Rawlinson's translation appears in Everyman's Library ; also Thucydides : Jowett's translation is the best, but there is one in Everyman. The first of these will show the kind of material from which the earlier history has to be reconstructed ; the second is itself one of the best ever written, and essential to a knowledge of Greek history. Grote's *History of Greece* is still the best in English (Everyman : 12 vols.), while for the fifth century, and especially the Athenian democracy, Routledge's abridged "Grote" (5s.), with excellent modern notes by Mitchell and Caspari, is invaluable. Bury's *History of Greece* (Macmillan : 8s. 6d.) is very good reading, but not entirely trustworthy ; Holm's *History* in 4 vols. (Macmillan), translated from the German, is very sound, and the 4th volume (separate, 7s. 6d.) is practically the only continuous account of the Greek world after the death of Alexander. Of works on special periods or subjects there may be mentioned Mahaffy's *Alexander's Empire* (Stories of the Nations), Freeman's *History of Sicily*, 4 vols., and Warde Fowler's *City State of the Greeks and Romans*, an interesting and illuminating work (Macmillan : 5s.). Alexander, Pericles, and Demosthenes are treated in Putnam's " Heroes of the Nations " series (5s. each).

For a thorough appreciation of Greek History a good Atlas is essential : Kiepert's *Classical Atlas* (5s.) is perhaps the best, and Murray's *Classical Atlas* (6s.) is also good ; that in Everyman is rather difficult to work with, but would be found useful.

INDEX.

THE END.

PRINTED IN GREAT BRITAIN AT
THE PRESS OF THE PUBLISHERS.

> " We have nothing but the highest praise for these little books, and no one who examines them will have anything else."—*Westminster Gazette.*

THE PEOPLE'S BOOKS

THE PEOPLE'S BOOKS—(Continued).